MW00954203

Pickling and Fermenting

for Beginners

The Complete Guide to Pickling and Fermenting with Easy Recipes for Quick, Fermented, and Sweet Pickles, Sauerkraut, Relishes, Pickled Meat, Fish, and Eggs, and Fermented Beverages

Max Barnes

2

© COPYRIGHT 2023 MAX BARNES - ALL RIGHTS RESERVED.

The content contained within this book may not be reproduced, duplicated or transmitted without direct written permission from the author or the publisher.

Under no circumstances will any blame or legal responsibility be held against the publisher, or author, for any damages, reparation, or monetary loss due to the information contained within this book. Either directly or indirectly.

Legal Notice:

This book is copyright protected. This book is only for personal use. You cannot amend, distribute, sell, use, quote or paraphrase any part, or the content within this book, without the consent of the author or publisher.

Disclaimer Notice:

Please note the information contained within this document is for educational and entertainment purposes only. All effort has been executed to present accurate, up to date, and reliable, complete information. No warranties of any kind are declared or implied. Readers acknowledge that the author is not engaging in the rendering of legal, financial, medical or professional advice. The content within this book has been derived from various sources. Please consult a licensed professional before attempting any techniques outlined in this book.

By reading this document, the reader agrees that under no circumstances is the author responsible for any losses, direct or indirect, which are incurred as a result of the use of the information contained within this document, including, but not limited to, — errors, omissions, or inaccuracies.

Your Free Gift

I'd like to offer you a gift as a way of saying thank you for purchasing this book. It's the eBook called A Beginner's Guide to Container Gardening. If you'd like to grow your own food, but you think it's impossible since you don't have a big garden or a lot of land, then container gardening could be a perfect solution for you. It's a practical gardening method for urban and suburban gardeners who want to grow their own food but have limited space, and it will allow you to grow an abundance of food without having a big garden or acres of land. You can get your free eBook by scanning the QR code below with your phone camera and joining our community. Alternatively, please send me an email to **maxbarnesbooks@gmail.com** and I will send you the free eBook.

SPECIAL BONUS!

Want this book for free?

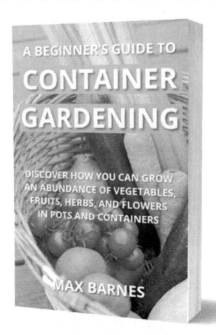

Get FREE unlimited access to it and all of my new books by joining our community!

Scan with your phone camera to join!

Contents

Introduction

There are lots of benefits to pickling and fermenting at home. Pickling and fermenting can help you preserve the food from your garden or a farmer's market that you're not able to consume immediately. It means that you get to eat the food you love not only when it's in season because pickling and fermentation help it last longer. Pickled and fermented food has a lovely taste, and there are so many options to make it varied and personalized using recipes from around the world that you can adapt to suit you. Pickling and fermenting also have wonderful health benefits. Pickled and fermented foods contain natural antioxidants, and fermented food has probiotics that can help your gut health. You control every step of the process, which means you can choose exactly which ingredients to put in and which to leave out. So, for example, if you love garlic but hate peppers—you can adapt the recipes accordingly. You personally control the pickling liquid strength, and you can tailor the recipe to create the perfect pickles for you.

Many people would like to start pickling and fermenting at home, but they often don't know where to start. Beginners can feel overwhelmed when they think about pickling and fermenting and can worry that it's too complicated or may have concerns that it's unsafe and that the food wouldn't be edible. These concerns are usually because they don't have the knowledge they need to pickle and ferment food or they've got information from poor quality sources. This book, however, will teach beginners everything they need to know about pickling and fermenting so that by the end of it you are a pickling and fermenting expert with a fridge and cupboards full of delicious jars of pickled and fermented food. Did you know that when Kate Middleton, the now Princess of Wales, wasn't sure what to buy the late Queen Elizabeth II as a present, she made the Queen a jar of chutney that followed her grandma's recipe? The Queen absolutely loved it and thought it was an incredibly considerate homemade gift, and she had it on her table the next day to eat with cheese and bread (Reddin, 2021, online). It was made from marrows, onions, apples, sultanas, dates, and pickling spice. You'll find similar chutney recipes that you could give as gifts to others in Chapter 7 of this book.

What This Book Will Cover

Throughout this book, you will learn about pickling and fermenting, the differences between them, how they work, different methods, plus the tools and supplies you require for your kitchen. You will discover two different acids you can use for fermentation, plus all about alcoholic fermentation, as well as primary or secondary fermentation.

You will find quick pickle recipes with a wide variety of foods you can swiftly pickle (my favorite is crunchy pickled cucumbers that are so delicious). These are easy and non-time consuming and give you great snacks in your fridge. There is a wide range of fermented pickle recipes to delight your tastebuds. There are recipes and techniques for fruit and sweet pickles (these are ideal if you have an apple tree, or grow your own cherry tomatoes, onions, or carrots, or have a good farmer's market nearby).

There is a chapter on how to make sauerkraut, kimchi, and other cabbage pickles—perfect accompaniments to hot dogs, schnitzels, grilled cheese sandwiches, soups, stews, noodles, savory pancakes, and meat dishes.

You will learn to make relish, chutneys, salsas, and other condiments (dips/spreads and sauces, including an amazing, tongue-tingling fermented hot sauce) so that you have the perfect accompaniment to sandwiches, burgers, wraps, curries, cheese, meat, salads, tacos, fajitas, and quesadillas, among many other things.

This book will show you how to pickle a wide variety of foods, including meat, fish, and eggs. The wonderful thing about pickling and fermenting is that it preserves food for so much longer, meaning there's much less food waste, and you get more for your money, plus you can use your homegrown food to much greater effect, leading to a more sustainable lifestyle. There are many countries in the world that are especially known for their pickling and fermentation techniques, including Germany, Poland, the

Netherlands, India, Korea, and Japan, so these cultures and others have been drawn upon to create some really interesting techniques and tasty, delicious recipes.

The book has a chapter on non-alcoholic fermented beverages, including the incredibly delicious kombucha tea, which is so good for digestion and ridding your body of toxins as well as boosting your energy and immune system. It can help you lose weight, reduce blood pressure, and lower the risk of heart disease and cancer. It contains other probiotic drinks, including kefir, which is excellent for gut health.

The final chapter of the book is on brewing alcohol and contains recipes for fermented alcoholic drinks.

Why I'm Writing This Book

My name is Max, and I grew up on a farm helping my grandmother Anna. Pickling and preserving produce from her farm and garden are among my first memories. Because I had small and nimble fingers, she used to get me to peel the skins off onions to get them ready for pickling. I also helped with peeling different vegetables and fruits for different chutneys and relishes. Lunch time at my grandma's was always a delight, with lovely jars of chutney and relish to accompany cheese, bread, quiche, salads, and more. We had some incredible picnics too. My grandmother always experimented with different pickling and fermenting recipes. She was well travelled and took influence from many different cultures.

I have retained my grandmother's love for pickling and fermenting, and I have continued doing this as an adult. My kitchen cupboards, shelves, and fridge are always full of neatly labelled jars containing family-favorite recipes that have been passed down through generations. I love the fact that it's another way to use up the abundance of vegetables and fruits that we grow on our homestead that helps us to live a sustainable lifestyle. All these pickles, chutneys, salsas, and sauces add some real pizazz to mealtimes, really bringing the best flavors of food. Doing pickling and fermenting always brings back fond memories of my childhood and helping my grandmother on her farm. This is where I learned many of the techniques. I have continued to experiment with different recipes and have expanded my knowledge from reading cookbooks, watching cooking shows from the world's greatest chefs, and trying recipes I've found on the Internet, and all this combined has allowed me to develop my own recipes that I've tweaked and honed until I'm 100% happy with how they taste.

I want to show people that pickling and fermenting are not as difficult as some people might think, and the benefits of doing this far outweigh the time, money, and effort invested. I think homemade pickles, relishes, and chutneys taste so much better than store-bought—they are so delicious, and you know every ingredient they contain.

In this book, I want to share some of my favorite recipes for pickling and fermenting. This book is a guide to pickling and fermenting different foods. It is not a guide to anything else outside the realm of pickling and fermenting.

So, without further ado, let's move to the first chapter, which is all about pickling. You'll learn what pickling is, how it works, the difference between pickling and fermentation, how to get started with pickling and different methods you could use, and the tools and supplies you require for your pickler's kitchen.

Chapter 1: Pickling 101

This chapter will explain exactly what pickling is and how it works. It will discuss the differences between pickling and fermentation. It will also cover the basics of pickling and different pickling methods that you can choose from. And finally, it will suggest pickling tools and supplies that will come in useful for your pickler's kitchen.

What is Pickling and How Does It Work?

Pickling is a technique that is used all around the world. In New York, you can find kosher cucumber pickles often served on the side to sandwiches in a deli. In the Southern United States, you'll find pickled pigs' feet. In India, there are chutneys to accompany curries. In Korea, there is kimchi that is added to soups, hotpots, or stirred through rice. There are miso pickles in Japan, known as tsukemoni, which accompany most traditional meals alongside rice and miso soup. In China, you will find salted duck eggs that are traditionally served with congee (rice porridge) for breakfast, but the salted duck egg yolks are also used in mooncakes, pastries, and zongzi (rice dumplings). In Scandinavia, there is pickled herring, and it's commonly served in a dish called S.O.S, which stands for "smör, ost och sill" and is butter and cheese with pickled herring—it's typically a starter in Swedish restaurants. Corned beef is a favorite dish in Ireland, always popular around St. Patrick's Day. Mexico makes great use of salsas, which are delicious to accompany tacos.

One of the key points that will be reinforced throughout the book is that the acidity in a pickled product is essential—not just for taste and texture but for safety reasons. You should never alter the proportions of vinegar, water, or food in a recipe because if it's not acidic enough, *Clostridium botulinum*, a bacterium that is toxic and can cause botulism, may appear in low acidic foods.

The key thing that defines a pickle is that it is something that prevents food from spoiling—it preserves the food and makes it last longer. It gives it a longer shelf life, often through marinating it in a form of brine or vinegar. Pickles are best made from young, fresh vegetables and fruits, vinegar, and fresh, whole spices and herbs.

Pickles can be preserved with vinegar or salt. Vinegar brine pickles use salt too, but unlike salt brine pickles, they are not fermented and don't have probiotics; however, they are easy and quick to make and are often called quick pickles. When you pickle with salty brine, however, it creates lactic acid, which works to preserve the food—this process is called lacto-fermentation. Despite its name, the term "lacto" has nothing to do with milk or lactose. Salt brine pickles are also called fermented pickles, and they have lots of probiotics or beneficial bacteria, which makes them really good for your gut health.

When making quick pickles, vinegar is usually heated with salt, sugar, and spices, such as mustard and garlic, to add flavor to the brine and to prevent bad bacteria from developing. The food to be pickled is placed in a jar, and the hot brine is added. Then the jar is sealed, and this preserves the food for a period of time. When you pickle food, it destroys yeast, mold, and bacteria that could cause the food to spoil, and it destroys enzymes that would impact the color, flavor, and texture of the produce.

Fermented pickles as well as differences between pickling and fermenting will be covered in more detail a bit later in this chapter, but in short, you would usually simply cover products that naturally contain lactic acid bacteria, such as cucumbers or cabbage, in a brine of water and salt as well as herbs and spices and then let them ferment for a few days in a sealed container.

Pickling and fermenting are something that has been around for hundreds of years, preserving food so that people have food to eat over long winters, famine, or other times of need. Over 2,000 years ago, the people who built the Great Wall of China were known to have eaten sauerkraut. During the Age of Discovery, sailors took a lot of pickled food to help feed them throughout their voyage (Chavis, 2022, online). Caesar fed pickles to his troops to improve their health and wellbeing, and Cleopatra thought that her beauty was in large part due to her diet that included fermented food (Houston, 2018, online).

Pickling can add spicy, sour, and acidic flavors to food, which makes it taste truly delicious as well as helps preserve it. Cucumbers are one of the most common foods to be pickled, but onions are another favorite. You can have pickled garlic and carrots. I adore pickled cauliflower and think it's delicious. You can pickle a lot of different vegetables and fruits as well as things like fish, beef, pork, sausages, eggs, and more.

When making vinegar brine pickles, the vinegar needs to have 5% acidity to cause the change in flavor, texture, and to be a preservative to the food. Distilled white vinegar and white wine vinegar are commonly used to pickle food because they don't impact the color of most vegetables. An exception to this are red onions, which turn pink in white vinegar.

Another common pickling liquid is cider vinegar, which is milder tasting, but can mean the food has a slightly darker color. The best salt to use when pickling is pickling (or canning) salt, which is pure, granulated, and does not contain anti-caking agents that can make your pickling liquid cloudy, or kosher salt, which has large crystals and can be a bit more difficult to use. If you use tap water that contains chlorine, this can interfere with the pickling process, but if it's drinkable, it's generally OK to use for pickling. The acid in the vinegar and natural acids in vegetables slow down the process of decay, and the salt preserves the crunchiness of the food.

Because pickling includes salt and water, pickles can help balance electrolytes in the body, which means they can be good to eat after you've been to the gym. They also have B vitamins, which give you energy and help with digestion (Chavis, 2022, online).

Differences between Pickling and Fermentation

While sometimes people use the terms "pickling" and "fermentation" interchangeably, they are very different. The methods used for both have some overlap, so it's easy to understand why people get confused. But in a nutshell, pickling does not include any fermentation—it's essentially just soaking the food in vinegar. Pickling with vinegar is a faster method than fermentation—it involves heating the acidic liquid, pouring it over the food, and placing it in a sealed container. The acidity in the vinegar will kill off bad bacteria and prevent the food from spoiling.

Pickling uses an acidic brine to preserve the food. Acidic brines can be made from salt water, sugar water, lemon juice, or vinegar. Whichever liquid is used, it is poured over vegetables, fruits, meat, or fish, which are then placed in a sealed jar for a number of days to let the liquid permeate the food and change its taste, usually by making it sour. Vinegar brined pickles are also called fresh pickles because they're not fermented (though they usually contain some salt). They may also be called quick pickles or refrigerator pickles.

As for fermentation, the difference between pickling and fermenting is that when you ferment something, the food is soaked in salt water solution, which encourages fermentation. Fermentation is a chemical reaction between sugars in the food and naturally present bacteria, so no acid is added. Usually, the sugars and carbohydrates in food are eaten by the good bacteria, and the sugar is converted into acids, carbon dioxide, and alcohol. These substances then preserve the food and enhance its flavor. Fermentation helps probiotics and other beneficial live bacteria to thrive, and these really aid digestion (these also don't exist in vinegar brined pickles). When you eat fermented food, this is great for a healthy diet.

One of the best-known examples of fermented food is sauerkraut—it's salted, shredded cabbage that has fermented. Kimchi is another fermented food. With kimchi and sauerkraut, the fermentation method draws water out of the produce using dry salt. The cabbage used in the dishes is maintained at room temperature to allow for fermentation and moisture to develop. Once done, they can be stored in jars.

For foods with a high water content, salting the produce helps to draw the water out, and this creates a brine, like with sauerkraut. This method is called natural fermentation or wild fermentation. You should use a proper fermentation vessel, like a fermentation crock, or as a beginner, you can purchase fermentation kits.

Fermented pickles are considered a type of pickle, but vinegar brine pickles are not fermented. So, sauerkraut is a type of pickle, but a vinegar brined dill is not fermented. Fermentation is also used in bread baking, where the yeast converts sugar to carbon dioxide and alcohol, which causes the dough to rise. It is also used to produce yogurt. Different types of fermentation will be covered in more detail in the next chapter.

Pickling Basics and Different Pickling Methods

It is important to ensure your containers that you're placing food in to pickle have been properly sterilized and have seals so that mold does not start to grow.

There are 3 main methods of pickling, which include:

1. Quick pickling
2. Salt brine pickling
3. Vinegar brine soak and rinse

Quick Pickling

Quick pickles (also known as fresh pickles or refrigerator pickles) have the entire Chapter 3 of this book devoted to them, so I'll only briefly explain what they are here. Essentially, you place whatever vegetables you want to pickle into sterilized jars. The vegetables can be sliced, chopped, or left whole. Then you cover the vegetables in pickling brine that has been boiled, which typically consists of vinegar, water, salt, sometimes sugar, as well as herbs and spices. Sometimes these can be refrigerated, other times you can use a water bath canning method to preserve them for longer. It can help to blanch or sometimes cook vegetables before pickling. Blanching is scalding vegetables in boiling water or steam for a short time. For example, you would blanch asparagus, and you would cook and cool beets. Vegetables that are great for quick pickling include cucumbers, carrots, green beans, peppers, and cauliflower. You can also quick pickle fruits, such as apples and cherries. Quick pickles are ready to eat in a few days. They may have a bit less depth to their flavor compared to fermented pickles, but they are a nice introduction for beginners to pickling. In the fridge, quick pickles tend to last anywhere from a few weeks to a few months. If you know you want to eat your pickles fairly quickly, this is a good method.

If vegetables are tough, like beets, you'll need to cook them prior to pickling, but others, like asparagus, should just be blanched. You'll need to cut them into pieces that easily fit in pickling jars. These could be disks, or spears, or some vegetables can be kept whole if they're bite sized. You'll need to add in seasonings of herbs and spices—usually about ½ teaspoon of spices and a couple of sprigs of herbs should be ideal for a standard jar. Typically, there should be equal parts of water and vinegar. Depending on what produce you're pickling, you may want sugar too. You will need to combine your vinegar, water, salt, sugar, and spices in a saucepan, bring it to a boil to dissolve the sugar and the salt, boil for 2 minutes, then remove it from the heat, and pour the brine in the jars over the produce until the vegetables or fruit are completely covered. Secure the jars with a lid, and ensure they are

refrigerated for at least 24 hours before you eat them. You do need to keep quick pickles in the fridge, and not on a shelf. They don't keep quite as long as canned or fermented pickles.

Salt Brine Pickling

Salt brine pickling is for vegetables that have a high water content, and you salt the vegetables before they are placed in jars, which will draw some of the water out and will allow the pickles to soak into the vegetables and give them more flavor and preserve them for longer. You can place vegetables into a wide non-metallic bowl, spread pickling salt on top, cover it, and let it sit overnight in the fridge. After salting, you drain and rinse them. Once the salt has drawn the water out, rinse and drain the product, then use the quick pickling method described above. Bread and butter pickles (also known as sweet and sour pickles), kosher dill pickles, cucumbers, eggplant, zucchini, and cabbage are commonly salt brined. Salt brined pickles have a lovely crunch to them.

Vinegar-Brine Soak and Rinse Method

This technique gets the most amount of water out of produce and allows vegetables to be completely saturated by pickling liquid. Essentially, you soak the vegetables in salt brine, like in the salt brine pickling method described above, then drain them, and then soak them again in a vinegar solution before you drain and rinse them. You will often find that 9-day or 12-day pickles as well as sweet gherkins are made using this technique. It can also be used to pickle watermelon rind, soft fruits, and sweet and sour gherkins.

Fermented Pickles

When you fermented pickles, the produce needs to be submerged in salt water brine, with weights to keep it submerged. They are usually kept at room temperature. You will need a pickling crock or a fermentation kit. The vegetables you submerge must never get any oxygen or bacteria from open air. They will ferment over days or weeks depending on the recipe you use, the environment you live in, and personal preferences.

During fermentation, the salt draws the water out of the vegetables, and microbes that occur naturally eat the sugar and create lactic acid and good bacteria. The pH of the liquid lowers, which helps preserve vegetables and keep them safe to eat. You do not add acid, vinegar, or sugar when fermenting. Fermented pickles have a distinctive flavor and smell that cannot be achieved through other methods, like quick pickling. Fermented pickles are the healthiest for you due to the beneficial live bacteria and probiotics created during fermentation (Mountain Feed, n.d, online). Sauerkraut and kimchi are some of the most well-known fermented pickle recipes. There is a piece of equipment that we'll look at in the next section called a fermentation crock or pickling crock, which is useful for fermenting.

Water Bath Canning Method

This is a canning method that helps preserve pickles for longer. With this method, jars with pickles are heated in a boiling water bath for a set amount of time. Hot water bath canning is used only for high acid food with pH values of 4.6 or lower. The acidity can be natural, like it is in most fruits, jams, and jellies, or added, like in pickled vegetables. Acidic foods contain enough acid to stop the growth or destroy botulism bacteria rapidly when heated. You can purchase a pH meter or pH strips to measure the acidity of your recipes.

You will need a boiling water canner or a large, deep saucepot with a lid, and a rack. You will need to purchase specific jars for water bath canning, such as Ball Mason jars. These types of jars have 2-piece lids, a round metal screw band, and a removable flat metal lid with a rubber seal. You can reuse canning jars, provided they are not chipped or rusty, but it is important to get new jar lids each year so that the seal is tight. Put the jars into a large pot of hot water (180°F or 82°C) prior to filling them. If you will be storing light sensitive products, you could purchase amber jars—these are great for fermented food.

You need to place the filled jars onto a rack in the canner that contains hot water—it should be deep enough to cover the jars by at least 1 inch (2.5 cm). It should then be brought to a boil, and you'll need to process the jars for however long the recipe says. If it does not give a time, then it needs to be processed for at least 10 minutes.

Food that has been processed in this way should be safe for 1 year. Once you open the jar, it should be refrigerated and treated like fresh food.

Some Tips Regarding the Type of Food to Pickle

If you're pickling cucumbers, ensure they are unwaxed because brine cannot permeate the wax. If you were to use table or slicing cucumbers, you would not get a good quality pickle. If you cut cucumbers into slices, you'll get a softer dill pickle. Cucumbers should be pickled within 24 hours of them being picked. They should be 1.5 inches (3.8 cm) in length for gherkins and 4 inches (10 cm) for dills. You need to wash them thoroughly, especially around the stem, to ensure there is no soil, which could contain bacteria. Blossoms contain enzymes that can cause softening, so you should remove the blossom end to stop the pickle from going soft—generally a 1/16-inch (1.5 mm) slice from the blossom end is enough. If vegetables have any mold on them, dispose of them, and do not use them for pickling. While pickling helps prevent spoilage, if vegetables already have mold on them, they may have an "off" taste.

With other vegetables, choose tender ones, and pickle them within 24 hours of picking. Make sure to wash them thoroughly before pickling. Research to find out whether you need to blanch the vegetables you'd like to pickle, pre-cook them, or just use them raw. This will be covered in the recipes later in the book, but just as an example, asparagus is blanched, beets need to be pre-cooked in their skins for 30 minutes, and things like green beans, carrots, onion, mushrooms, and zucchini should be pickled raw. It is best to use white distilled vinegar for onions and cauliflower so that the vinegar doesn't taint the color of the vegetables. If you want to pickle fruits, you may want to select pears and peaches that are slightly underripe for pickling.

Pickling Tools and Supplies

If you're just starting out and want to do quick pickling, then you will need a saucepan or a pot, a heat source, and some airtight jars. This makes quick pickling a fun and inexpensive hobby to try. You will need to wash the jars in soapy water, rinse them well, and keep them hot. If you're going to use your jars and they won't be placed in a boiling water canner for more than 10 minutes, then the jars should be sterilized by boiling them for 10 minutes before being filled.

For quick pickles, you can heat your pickling liquid in a stainless steel, glass, or enamel saucepan. This is often termed in recipes and cookbooks as non-reactive cookware, and this means you shouldn't use copper, brass, aluminum, galvanized, or iron utensils because these metals can react with acids or salts and cause your brine to have a color and/or flavor you don't want. Foods that have been cooked in aluminum can oxidize and go black and have a metallic tang. This applies to any utensils you use too because you don't want acids or salts to change the color or taste of your pickles. One of my favorite things to use to cook pickles is a 5- or 8-quart enameled cast iron Dutch oven, like a Le Creuset. For short term brining or soaking you can use crocks, saucepans, or bowls from stoneware, glass, or stainless steel.

You will need some measuring cups and/or a kitchen scale to be able to have the exact weight of items for recipes. You may need a funnel to get your produce neatly into your jars. You can purchase canning funnels that allow you to pour your produce and pickling liquid into jars with ease. Some funnels also come with strainers, which can be useful.

You may also want a jar lifter to get jars out of hot water after sterilizing or processing. You may want to get a bubble popper, which helps let out any excess air that may be inside the jar, and some of these also let you measure the headspace on the jar so that you create a sufficient vacuum seal. You could buy a jar wrench that allows you to officially seal the jar after a water bath, and it can also be used to open tight jars, which can be helpful to people who may struggle with hand mobility/strength. You will also want some kitchen towels, sponges, and cloths to clear up after you're done filling your delicious jars of pickles and chutney. Having labels for your jars so that you can neatly label and date them is good too.

You will need a boiling water canner to process pickles that you intend to store at room temperature.

With time, if you'd like to get more into pickling, you can expand and get a crock (these can also be called fermentation or pickling crocks) to do fermentation.

You will also need containers and weights for fermentation. Sauerkraut can be fermented in a large stoneware crock, large glass jars, or food grade plastic containers (check the label or consult with the manufacturer to ensure the containers are food grade). Don't ever use aluminum, copper, brass, galvanized, or iron containers to ferment pickles or sauerkraut. There needs to be at least 2 inches (5 cm) of space between the food and the top of the container—this is often called headspace, and this is needed so that you get a strong seal on the lid. If you want to ferment

5 lb (2.3 kg) of fresh vegetables, you would require a 1-gallon (3.8L) container. When you're fermenting, you need to ensure the vegetables are covered with brine at all times, so you can use a heavy plate or a glass lid to keep them fully submerged.

Airtight Jars

These need to be secure in order to keep your pickles fresh and prevent your fridge from smelling of vinegar. Ball Mason quart jars are ideal for this. If you don't have the budget to go and buy new jars, then you can recycle existing glass jars. You'll need to sterilize them well and wash them to remove their existing labels/glue. We also use coffee jars as well as marmalade and jam jars, and they all work just fine. If you have a selection of different sized jars, try to match the food to the jar—for example, you can put asparagus spears and beans in taller jars and relishes in smaller jars. If you give your chutneys and pickles to family, ask them to return the jars afterwards.

To sterilize jars, you need to heat them to a point where no bacteria could survive. It's best to sterilize them immediately before pickling. You also need to sterilize spoons, funnels, and utensils. Everything

needs to be clean so that no bad bacteria spoil your pickles.

You can sterilize jars in the oven (if your jars have rubber seals, remove them before placing them in the oven). Preheat the oven to 130°F (55°C) (higher temperatures can crack jars). Wash the jars and lids in hot soapy water. Rinse them in hot water, don't dry them, but instead put them in the pre-heated oven on a tray lined with baking paper, and leave them there for 20 minutes. You can wash the lids in hot water while the jars are in the oven. Let your jars cool to room temperature before putting anything in them. You can also purchase a lid lifter tool, which is a pen with a magnet at the end that lets you lift the lid without touching it. This can help get lids easily out of boiling water and keep them sterile and untouched by hands.

If you have a dishwasher, you can sterilize your pickling jars on the highest temperature setting. Don't have other dirty dishes in the machine at the same time because they can contaminate your pickling jars. You can include the rubber seals from the jars in a dishwasher.

If you have a microwave, you can put your clean jars into a microwave for 45 seconds to sterilize them. You can rinse them in hot water first and leave them a little wet. Don't put any metal clips or lids in the microwave.

For fresh pickles or refrigerator pickles that you intend to keep in the fridge for a while, you need to keep an eye on the lids and loosen them every few days because the bacteria will start the fermentation process, and carbon dioxide will build up inside, increasing the pressure inside the jars, so you need to "burp" them to let the excessive pressure out. There's no need

to remove the lids—just gently unscrew the lid or tug the tab on the rubber seal, and this will allow just enough gas to escape.

For water bath canning, you will need to purchase specific jars, such as Ball Mason jars. These types of jars have 2-piece lids, a round metal screw band, and a removable flat metal lid with a rubber seal. You can reuse canning jars, provided they are not chipped or rusty, but it is important to get new jar lids each year so that the seal is tight. Put the jars into a large pot of hot water (180°F or 82°C) prior to filling them. If you will be storing light sensitive products, you could purchase amber jars—these are great for fermented food.

Vinegar

Follow the recipes precisely, and don't change the proportions of vinegar, water, and produce. Do not use a vinegar if you're unsure of how acidic it is—it should have 5% acetic acid (50 grain). Do not dilute vinegar because it prevents bad bacteria from growing.

There are different types of vinegar you can use. Most people use distilled white vinegar (fermented from pure alcohol), which won't impact the color of your vegetables—this is ideal for onions, cauliflower, and pears. But you can also use apple cider vinegar (fermented from hard apple cider), apple cider flavored distilled vinegar, and rice wine vinegar. Some English pickles, like pickled onions, use malt vinegar (also known as brown vinegar), which is fermented from sprouted barley. You can look for the perfect vinegar for your produce. Balsamic vinegar is good for onions, and malt vinegar is perfect for eggs.

If you used vinegars with only 3 or 4% acidity, this is not safe enough for home pickling. Do not use salad vinegar or wine vinegars (made from wine grapes) unless they're 5%, and do not use homemade vinegar. If you want your pickles to taste less sour, never dilute the vinegar—add more sugar instead.

Pickling/Canning Salt

You should use pickling or canning salt for pickling and ensure that it does not contain iodine or anti-caking agents because they can make your brine cloudy. Avoid salt with additives. You can purchase pickling or canning salt from a supermarket, a hardware store, or a farm supply store. Pickling or canning salt is essentially pure salt—granulated sodium chloride—without any additives, such as anti-caking agents. You can also use sea salt or kosher salt.

As for fermenting, you can use the same types of salt as for pickling, but I personally prefer using sea salt.

Do not use table salt or iodized salt for pickling and fermenting because these contain potassium iodine, dextrose, and may have additives, like calcium silicate and sodium aluminosilicate, which are anti-caking agents. If you're unsure what type of salt you have, stir some in a glass of water. If it's cloudy, this isn't good for your pickling liquid.

Sugar

Use white sugar unless the recipe tells you to use a different type of sugar. However, you could try brown sugar, honey, or agave syrup for a different flavor. Sugar helps keep pickles plump and firm.

Spices and Herbs

Wherever possible, use fresh whole spices because these will give your pickles the best taste. If you use powdered spices, this may darken the brine and vegetables. Classic pickling spices and herbs often include whole peppercorns, mustard seed, coriander seed,

chilies, allspice, bay leaves, dill, red pepper flakes, and jalapenos. You could also include a few slices of onion, lemon, lime, ginger, or galangal. Think about what type of food you would like your pickle to accompany.

A really good tip is that pickles will become less dark if you tie whole spices loosely in a clean white cloth or a cheesecloth bag, boil the bag with your brine, and then remove it before pouring the brine into jars. Another good tip is that you could use a cabbage leaf or a vine leaf on top of your pickled vegetables to stop them from floating to the surface and being exposed to air. It will help your pickles retain their crisp crunch.

How to Make Your Own Pickling Spice

You will notice that many recipes call for pickling spice. While you can purchase it in a supermarket, it is super easy to make your own—pickling spice is just essentially a spice blend. Most basic pickling spices always include mustard seed, peppercorns, and bay leaves, and depending on what's being pickled, more aromatics can be added. The best thing about making your own pickling spice is that you can add the ingredients you like and leave out the ones you're not so keen on.

I personally use the following base ingredients when making homemade pickling spice:

- Dill seed
- Mustard seed
- Coriander seed
- Whole black peppercorns
- Allspice berries
- Red chili flakes
- Bay leaves

You can experiment and add other spices to your blend, such as:

- Cardamom seeds
- Star anise
- Whole cloves
- Celery seeds
- Cinnamon sticks
- Dried ginger
- Fennel seeds
- Juniper berries

Below you find a recipe for making homemade pickling spice that I personally use:

Ingredients

- 2 tablespoons dill seed
- 2 tablespoons mustard seed
- 2 tablespoons coriander seed
- 2 tablespoons black peppercorns
- 1 tablespoon allspice berries
- 1 teaspoon crushed red pepper flakes

- 10–12 dried bay leaves, crumbled

Instructions

1. Simply add of the ingredients to a small bowl and stir to mix.
2. As mentioned previously, you can experiment and add or leave out different ingredients.

Dill

Dill is often added to jars of pickles before the brine is added. If you decide to add dill, ensure that it's clean, fresh, and that there are no insects on it. While you can use frozen dill, it's not as good as fresh. You can add one and a half heads of dill per quart (0.95L). If you only have seeds, you can substitute 1 tablespoon of dill seed for 1 head of dill.

Garlic

Garlic is usually added to jars of pickles before the brine is added if the recipe calls for this. Be wary of how much garlic or hot peppers you add because this can lessen the acidity of your pickles and make them unsafe, so always follow the recipe carefully.

Distilled, Purified, or Filtered Water

Using distilled, purified, or filtered water will prevent your brine from looking cloudy. If you have hard water that contains a lot of minerals, this can interfere with the acidity and may stop your pickles from curing as they should. If your water has a lot of calcium, your pickles may shrivel. And if your water contains a lot of iron, your pickles may go dark in color. You can soften hard water by boiling it for 15 minutes and letting it settle for 24 hours, then draining off the sediment. You should add 1 tablespoon of vinegar per gallon of water (3.8L) before using it.

You can reuse brine if it hasn't been combined with vegetables to pickle. But don't reuse brine that has been mixed with vegetables because vegetables soak up the brine, which makes the brine less acidic, and this may mean the brine is not safe to pickle other vegetables. You don't want anyone to become sick because of food that was improperly canned, preserved, or fermented.

Produce

Cucumbers are often a good thing to try when you're starting out with pickling. Other things that are relatively easy to pickle include peppers, tomatoes, green beans, beets, cauliflower, onions, radishes, asparagus, carrots, jalapenos, and mushrooms. You can also pickle fruits and berries, such as apples, pears, peaches, cherries, strawberries, blueberries, and more.

Firming Agents

If your ingredients are fresh and good quality, you shouldn't really need to use any firming agents. You can soak cucumbers or other vegetables in ice water or crushed ice for 4–5 hours prior to pickling (sometimes a salt solution is added too).

It is best not to add alum nowadays. While alum was added in old pickling recipes, allegedly to make pickles crispier, if you eat a lot of it, it can make you feel sick and cause issues with your digestive system.

You can use pickling lime to help keep your pickles crispy, but I would suggest using calcium chloride instead. It will give you a nice crispness, and it's safer and easier to use than pickling lime. With pickling lime, you need to soak vegetables in it for 12–24 hours and then soak them in water for 1 hour at least 3 times (soak them for an hour each time. This is necessary because lime is alkaline and can lower the acidity of the brine. Calcium chloride does not lower acidity, so it's much safer and also easier to use—you simply need to ¼ teaspoon per quart (0.95L) jar of pickles before sealing the lid. Calcium chloride may add a bit of a salty taste, but it doesn't contain any sodium. When you purchase calcium chloride, it will last forever, but it's good to keep it dry because it will clump if it's humid.

You can also use grape leaves because these contain tannins, which stop pickles from going soft, or you can cut 1/16 inch (1.5 mm) off the blossom end of a cucumber instead of using these.

Water Baths

You need to ensure that any microorganisms that could spoil your pickles are destroyed, and using a water bath is a key way to do this. It will depend on what you're pickling, the acidity of the solution, and size of the jar to determine how long the water bath should last for, but typically it's between 10 and 30 minutes. I like to use a large, deep pot that holds at least 12 quarts (11.3L). It's an excellent canning kettle, stainless steel and non-reactive, and it's useful beyond being a water bath for other dishes. Your water bath or canning kettle needs a rack in its base because you don't want the jars to jangle together and crack. If it doesn't have a rack of its own, you can use a cake rack with feet. If you don't have one of these, you can use a folded kitchen towel at the base of the pot to give the jars some cushion.

I remember watching my grandma pickle homegrown cucumbers when I was a little kid. I helped her pick the cucumbers off the vines growing up the trellises in the garden. I then helped my grandma wash them thoroughly, ensuring there were no bits of soil or insects on them. Then she would pickle them with herbs and spices. They were quick pickles that were ready to eat the next day and were fantastic to use in cucumber and cream cheese sandwiches.

My grandma used equal amounts of white distilled vinegar and water and some pickling salt. She also added some whole coriander seed, whole mustard seed, peppercorn, and bay leaves. My grandma grew Kirby cucumbers, which are small and have bumpy skin. She would slice the cucumbers and put them in a colander with some ice cubes for 20 minutes, then drain them and pat them before pickling to give them extra crunch. The herbs and spices that she added to the pickling jars included dill, garlic, onions (chopped up), and whole or sliced peppers. To 1¼ pounds (560 g) of cucumbers, she added 3 cups (720 ml) of vinegar, 3 cups (720 ml) of water, 2½ tablespoons of pickling salt, and 1 tablespoon each of whole coriander seed, mustard seed, and peppercorns, plus 2 bay leaves. She would heat the pickling liquid until it boiled, then lower the heat for 10 minutes, and then put this to one side until it cooled. I then helped her put the cucumber slices in the jars along with the spices, and then my grandma would pour in the brine until they were all covered. She then put the lids on, always tapped the lids to get rid of air bubbles, then put them in the fridge.

We would always eat some the next day, but they definitely improved in flavor over the next few days. I helped my grandma with pickling so often, and I really remember the smell of the vinegar and spices, the enjoyment that I had doing it, and the pleasure of eating home-grown, home-pickled produce all year round. As such, I view pickling and fermenting with nostalgia and fondness, remembering lovely moments spent with my grandma. I learned a lot of different pickling and fermenting recipes from her over the years and have continued to learn and tweak them, which has culminated in me producing this book to pass on my knowledge to you to make things easy for a beginner to pickling and fermenting.

Key takeaways from this chapter:

1. Pickling is found in cultures around the world.

2. The acidity in pickles is important to prevent botulism.

3. It is best to use young, fresh vegetables and fruits and whole herbs and spices when pickling.

4. Many vegetables and fruits can be pickled, including cucumbers, garlic, carrots, cauliflower, asparagus, and much more. You can also pickle meat, sausages, fish, and eggs.

5. Distilled white vinegar is the most commonly used vinegar for pickling, as it doesn't change the color of pickled vegetables.

6. You should use pickling or canning salt, which doesn't contain any anti-caking agents or iodine.

7. Pickling uses an acidic brine made with vinegar, salt water, sugar water, or lemon juice. The acidic liquid helps preserve food and makes it taste sour.

8. Pickling and fermentation are not the same thing, although there are fermented pickles that use fermentation as part of the preparation process. Fermentation is where food is soaked in salt initially with no acid added. Fermentation is the reaction between the sugars in the food and the good bacteria, which are turned into acids, carbon dioxide, and alcohol. Fermented food has probiotics that are good for digestion.

9. Vinegar brine pickles are known as fresh pickles, quick pickles, or refrigerator pickles.

10. Quick pickles are vegetables covered in brine made with vinegar, water, salt, herbs, and spices that have been boiled—they are ready to eat in a few days.

11. Slat brine pickling involves salting vegetables to draw out the water, then using the quick pickling method.

12. Vinegar-brine soak and rinse method involves salting the vegetables, draining them, then soaking them in vinegar, and finally, draining and rinsing them.

13. With fermented pickles, the pickles are submerged under a salt water brine at room temperature, usually in a fermentation crock. They ferment over days or weeks, creating lactic acid and good bacteria.

14. You can use the water bath canning method to process pickled jars to keep them safe on shelves for a year (until opened, then refrigerate).

15. Remove the blossom end of cucumbers to prevent them from becoming soft.

16. Use non-reactive pans for pickling (you can use stainless steel, glass, or enamel cookware, but not copper, brass, aluminum, galvanized, or iron) because metals can react with the acids and salts in pickles.

17. Leave some space at the top of the pickling jar (known as headspace) so that you have an adequate seal on your lid.

18. You can sterilize glass jars in the oven, dishwasher, or microwave.

19. Replace jar lids every year so the seal is tight, and never reuse lids.

20. Vinegar should have 5% acetic acid to ensure safety.

21. Use fresh whole spices in your pickles.

22. Place a cabbage leaf or a vine leaf at the top of the pickling jar to prevent pickles floating to the surface.

23. Use distilled, purified, or filtered water when pickling. This will help avoid minerals affecting your pickles.

24. Never reuse brine if it's had vegetables in it.

25. Don't use alum or pickling lime when pickling—you can use calcium chloride or grape leaves if you need to.

26. When you place pickle jars in a water bath, you should leave them there for 5–30 minutes. Use a rack, a cake stand, or a kitchen towel at the base of the water bath to stop the jars jangling.

The next chapter will cover fermentation—what it is and how it works. Three types of fermentation will be discussed, including lactic acid, acetic acid, and alcoholic fermentation. Also, primary and secondary fermentation will be explored. This chapter will give you a thorough basic introduction to the most important things you need to know about fermenting.

Chapter 2: Fermentation 101

Fermented food is tasty, healthy, and it's not difficult to make. Because I live on a homestead, it's a great way to make the most of all the food we grow here by preserving it, which helps us live as sustainably as possible. You can start out using what you have in your kitchen, and if you develop a strong love of fermenting as I have, you can add more specialist equipment as the need arises.

Even if you live in an apartment in a busy city, fermenting is something that you can do at home. Fermented food and drinks are on trend—kimchi is one of the hottest food trends, and people love drinking "booch", which is a slang term for kombucha. Also, you'll find fermented hot sauces are very popular currently too.

What Is Fermentation and How Does It Work?

Fermentation extracts energy from carbohydrates (sugars or starch) without using oxygen. During the fermentation process, things like carbon dioxide, lactic acid, and ethanol may be produced. Yeast converts sugar into alcohol, and bacteria convert it into lactic acid. It is a metabolic process—living organisms consume carbohydrates (sugars/starch) and produce alcohol or acid. The alcohol or acid preserves food and gives it a distinctive tangy taste. Sometimes fungi may be involved (in things like miso).

During the fermentation process, sugars are converted into pyruvic acid while the glycolysis process is occurring. Without oxygen being present, pyruvic acid is converted into lactate via lactic acid or into carbon dioxide and ethanol via alcohol. People have been fermenting food for centuries, and fermentation is used to produce a wide variety of foods, like cheese, wine, sauerkraut, kombucha, yogurt, and much more. Fermented food creates probiotics, which have numerous health benefits, including aiding good digestion and building up your immune system.

The probiotics in fermented food can restore friendly bacteria in your gut, and this can help with things like irritable bowel syndrome (IBS) by reducing bloating, gas, constipation, and diarrhea. The bacteria in your gut impact your immune system, and therefore, probiotics can boost it and lessen your chances of getting sick. Fermented foods create an acidic environment in your gut, which can help get rid of harmful pathogens. If you're recovering from an illness, probiotics can help you recover more quickly. Often fermented foods contain vitamin C, iron, and zinc, all of which help your immune system too (Coyle, 2020, online).

Fermented food is broken down, which means it is easier to digest. Lactose is broken down into glucose and galactose, so even people who are lactose intolerant can generally drink kefir and eat yogurt. Fermentation can also break down phytates and lectins that occur in nuts, grains, seeds, and legumes, which can make it difficult for nutrients to be absorbed. When these are broken down, you're less likely to suffer from any mineral deficiencies. The probiotics *Lactobacillus helveticus* and *Bifidobacterium longum* (both found in fermented food) may help to reduce symptoms of anxiety and depression. Other probiotics, like *Lactobacillus rhamnosus* and *Lactobacillus gasseri,* have been linked to weight loss and reduced stomach fat. Fermented foods may lower the risk of heart disease, reduce blood pressure, and lower bad cholesterol (LDL) levels (Coyle, 2020, online).

Fermentation is also good for your mental health, and this is because your gut and brain are connected through the hypothalamic-pituitary-adrenal (HPA) axis, also known as the enteric nervous system. Simply speaking, how we feel in our gut can have an impact on our emotions. Serotonin—a hormone that makes us feel happy—is produced in the gut. When we have bad bacteria in our gut, they feed on sugar, and this can cause stress, bloating, and other gastrointestinal issues. If you can cut out some sugar and introduce some fermented foods to your diet, this can create good gut health and make you happy and healthy as a result (Plantables, online, 2019).

Fermented foods include:

- Sauerkraut (fermented shredded cabbage—it contains fiber and vitamins C and K, it has antioxidants for good eye health, and can also help prevent cancer—unpasteurized is best because pasteurization can kill good bacteria)

- Kimchi (fermented cabbage or radishes that can lower cholesterol, reduce insulin resistance, and cholesterol levels)

- Miso (fermented soybeans which can reduce risk of breast cancer and stokes, lower blood pressure, and are beneficial for heart health)

- Tempeh (this is made from fermented soybeans pressed into a cake to make a high protein meat substitute that contains antioxidants and can reduce heart disease and lower bad cholesterol (LDL) levels)

- Natto (also made from fermented soybeans—it has a strong taste and a slimy consistency, contains fiber and vitamin K, and it can prevent bone loss and blood clots and reduce high blood pressure)

- Kombucha (fermented tea which can prevent liver toxicity, reduce risk of cancer, and lower blood sugar and bad cholesterol (LDL) levels)

- Kefir (kefir grains are added to milk to create a thick, tangy beverage—this can help decrease inflammation and boost bone health)

- Yogurt (contains calcium, potassium, phosphorus, riboflavin, and vitamin B12—it may help reduce blood pressure, help with bone density, and prevent weight gain)

- Cheese

- Salami

- Olives

- Sourdough bread

- Beer

- Wine

Types of Fermentation

Lactic Acid Fermentation

This is where yeast and bacteria convert starch or sugar into lactic acid, which is a natural preservative. This commonly occurs in foods like sauerkraut, kimchi, pickles, yogurt, and sourdough bread (sourdough bread uses both lactic acid fermentation and alcoholic fermentation). This is the most common type of fermentation. It doesn't need heat for the fermentation to occur. It is an anaerobic chemical reaction, meaning it does not require oxygen.

Lactic acid is essential for preserving food. With kimchi or sauerkraut, cabbage is submerged in a salty brine, and the salt kills bad bacteria that would normally cause food to spoil, but it doesn't harm the *Lactobacillus* bacteria, and they convert the carbohydrates in the cabbage into lactic acid. The lactic acid preserves the cabbage and gives it a nice tangy flavor. Other foods, like tofu, miso, soy sauce, ketchup and pepperoni, are also made using lactic acid fermentation.

Alcoholic Fermentation

Alcoholic fermentation, also known as ethanol fermentation, is used to produce alcoholic beverages, such as beer, wine, and sprits, as well as bread (sourdough bread uses a combination of lactic acid and alcoholic fermentation). This is where pyruvate molecules in starch or sugar are broken down by yeast into ethyl alcohol and carbon dioxide. Oxygen is not required for this reaction to happen. Beer and wine have two stages of fermentation—primary and secondary—which will be discussed in the next section.

Acetic Acid Fermentation

Some people consider this to be another type of fermentation, although arguably, it is a version of ethyl alcohol fermentation This is where sugars or starches from grains or fruits are converted into sour-tasting vinegar or condiments—things like apple cider vinegar, wine vinegar, or kombucha. During acetic acid fermentation, acetic acid bacteria oxidize alcohol and sugar to form acetic acid, which is then used to make vinegar when diluted (white vinegar typically has 5% acetic acid content, and that's what's most commonly used for pickling).

Primary and Secondary Fermentation

When you start making homemade wine or beer, you will come across terms "primary fermentation" and "secondary fermentation". Despite the name, this does not mean you have to ferment your brew twice—these are just the stages of the fermentation process. Primary fermentation is a brief stage, and it begins as soon as you add yeast to juice (when making wine) or wort (when making beer). The yeast will start eating the sugar in the juice or wort and producing alcohol. In this stage, the yeast population is growing rapidly, and there will be a lot of visible activity. You will see a lot of foaming and lots of bubbles in your airlock. This is because primary fermentation is the most active and productive phase of fermentation due to all the sugar the yeast has to eat.

Secondary fermentation is the longer stage of fermentation that can last for days or weeks. The yeast will start to die off due to rising alcohol content, and there will be less sugar for the yeast to survive on. When the alcohol content reaches 12–15%, this will kill the yeast off, which prevents it from fermenting any further. If a greater level of fermentation is required, distillation needs to take place to remove water, which condenses the alcohol and gives a higher alcohol percentage.

With wine making, for example, primary fermentation starts the second you add yeast, and this is the stage where the yeast population is growing rapidly. There will be lots of visible activity—you may have foam on top of your wine, and your airlock will have lots of bubbles. The yeast grows fast because it has lots of sugar and oxygen at this point. This first stage typically lasts 3–5 days.

In the secondary fermentation stage, things slow down, the oxygen is depleted, and most of the sugar has been used. The yeast no longer expands, and some of it has died. Because alcohol content has risen, this makes it hard for the yeast to survive. Unused, dead yeast will fall to the bottom of the container. Secondary fermentation typically lasts 1–2 weeks when making wine. In this stage, foam will disappear, and bubbles will appear at the surface of your wine.

When you brew beer, fermentation occurs when the yeast converts malt sugar into ethyl alcohol. Primary fermentation will take place within 3–5 days, where the yeast eats most of the sugar (60–70% of it) and turns it into ethanol. The temperature of the beer will rise by 2–5°F (1–3°C), and the beer may have some fruity "off" smells, which are called phenols, during this time. You will see the yeast tumbling and swirling the liquid in this stage. Primary fermentation can produce a lot of carbon dioxide, so don't keep whatever you're fermenting in a closed room with no ventilation, as this would be dangerous. If you're brewing in a 5-gallon (19L) glass bottle, you will need a tube attached to it to deal with some of the dead yeast, proteins, and foam that is produced naturally. If you brew in a plastic bottle, you need to ensure the container has an airlock.

Secondary fermentation with beer is much calmer because the yeast has mostly done its job now. Some yeast will die and sink to the bottom of the container. You can transfer the beer to another sterilized vessel (ideally glass) at this point, and it will remove any dead yeast cells at the bottom of the container and just leave healthy yeast in the liquid. You won't need a plastic tube anymore because fermentation is slow in this stage. Secondary fermentation will take another 1–2 weeks (or sometimes even longer), and the yeast works more slowly in this stage.

Fermentation Basics

It may sound obvious, but it's similar to the advice given to people new to vegetable gardening, that you need to grow the vegetables you and your family like, or else no one will enjoy them. It's the same with fermenting vegetables—pick the vegetables your family likes. My family loves sauerkraut, tomatoes, cucumbers, carrots, bell peppers, and cauliflower, so I pickle a lot of those.

Sometimes vegetables will bleed their color into the brine. A key example of this is red cabbage, which will turn the brine pink. The cabbage itself may become quite dull and colorless, but this is all perfectly normal and is nothing to be concerned about.

The fresher produce you use, the better quality the end product will be. If you can, opt for fresh, seasonal vegetables. It's best to use filtered water, but if you don't have easy access to filtered water, you can boil tap water for 15 minutes and leave it in an open container for 24 hours so that chlorine can evaporate. Measure ingredients to ensure accuracy. Use salt that doesn't have additives or chemicals, like iodine or anti-caking agents. You can use pickling, pure, sea, or kosher salt—I personally prefer using sea salt for fermenting. With regards to how much salt to add, if you're using shredded vegetables, then you could put in 1 tablespoon of salt per quart (0.95L) of water. If you're using large vegetables, then use 2 tablespoons of salt per quart (0.95L) of water. When it comes to doing fermented pickles or sauerkraut, do not alter the concentrations of salt because proper fermentation is reliant upon these correct proportions. The fermentation needs to take place in anaerobic conditions (without oxygen), so ensure the container is airtight. The ideal temperature for fermentation should be between 65–72°F (18–22°C), and the container shouldn't be placed in direct sunlight.

When you're fermenting, you can add in some chopped onion, herbs, sliced garlic, or ginger. With time, you will learn what you do and don't like the flavor of. You can prepare vegetables how you want—you can grate, shred, chop, slice, or leave them whole—that is up to you. However, some vegetables are better suited to being left whole, and others grated. When you're fermenting, you will need to check the recipe and see whether you need salt, salt and drain, or a starter culture depending on what you're fermenting. Some vegetables that are often fermented include cabbage, green beans, carrots, tomatoes, hot peppers, garlic, onions, beets, and cauliflower. You're not limited to these, of course—these are just some of the choices. You can choose from a great variety of vegetables to ferment—the list is lengthy, and it's easier to state which aren't such a good choice, and that would include potatoes and broccoli.

When you ferment, it does need to be in an anaerobic environment, so your vegetables must be completely submerged in brine, and the container must have an airtight lid. If you spot any brown spots on your vegetables, mold, slime, or an off smell, then this is a sign that your vegetables have been exposed to oxygen, and it's best to throw them away immediately (you can compost them).

You will need a container big enough to hold the vegetables or fruits you intend to ferment—you could use a crockpot, glass jars, containers, or an ice cream bucket. Ball Mason jars and Kilner jars are perfect for fermenting, but sterilized old food jars will work too. A fermenting water-sealed crock is good for sauerkraut or large batches of vegetables. You will need a weighing stone or a plate with some weight to keep vegetables submerged in brine. A Tupperware shaker insert can fit well in jars to keep vegetables submerged. You can also use a plastic bag filled with water to keep vegetables down. Airtight jars are good, but you can also purchase seal-tight jars from Ikea that work very well, and they allow the air to vent (burp) when required. You can purchase fermentation kits, which typically contain fermentation lids with airlocks (so you won't have to burp your jars daily) and fermentation weights. These are great but not 100% necessary when you're first starting out.

You can ferment vegetables in their own brine or in water brine. Watery vegetables, such as radishes, shredded carrots, cucumbers, and more, can be fermented in their own brine. The most well-known recipe where vegetables are fermented in their own brine is sauerkraut. Salt draws juices out of cabbage, so you don't need to add any water.

Fermenting in water brine works best for vegetables that don't give off a lot of moisture, such as cauliflower, green beans, sliced carrots, and more. If you are fermenting using water brine, it's best to use filtered water rather than tap water because it may contain chemicals, like chlorine.

To ferment bigger chunks of vegetables, you should chop them into bite-sized pieces and fill the jar, leaving 1 inch of space (2.5 cm) at the top. Mix a quart (0.95L) of water with 1½ tablespoons of pickling, pure, sea, or kosher salt, and pour this over the vegetables. You can add flavors to your brine with things like dill, rosemary, garlic, ginger, turmeric, mustard seed, cinnamon, and pepper. You can add grape leaves or horseradish (just the stem of the leaf or the root) to keep your fermented vegetables crisp. Try to remove air bubbles with a butter knife. Then place a cabbage leaf on top of the vegetables to hold them all down under the brine. Cover the jar with an airtight lid. Then you simply need to wait. Not much will happen the first few days. But after that, the vegetables will become dull, and bubbles will appear at the top of the jar on top of the brine, and you'll see some bubbles among the vegetables too.

If you have a normal lid (and not a fermentation lid with an airlock), you'll need to burp the jar daily to release carbon dioxide buildup. You can twist the lid until you hear or feel the pressure releasing. Don't remove the whole lid, as this will allow air to get in. Just twist the lid swiftly to release pressure, then tighten it again.

You can ferment vegetables for 3–4 days before putting them in the fridge. Because fermented products can sometimes spill, you can stand the jar in a bowl so that it catches anything and saves making a mess. Fermenting most vegetables for 3–4 days is usually enough, but it depends on the recipe, and some recipes may require fermenting for a week or even more. Placing things in the fridge would stop the fermentation process, but if the jars are stored in a cellar, the fermentation process will continue but very slowly. Some people suggest not throwing out the brine after you've eaten your fermented vegetables, but instead drinking a few tablespoons a day to give you wonderful probiotics. I've been doing this ever since I started fermenting decades ago, and it always makes me feel great.

It's really important not to expose fermented food to air because it won't ferment properly and will spoil, which could give you food poisoning (botulism). Ways to avoid this include completely submerging the food in brine, using fermentation lids with airlocks, and using storage jars with good seals to prevent any air contamination.

Chapter 4 includes a variety of different recipes for fermenting various vegetables, and you will also find fermenting recipes throughout the book in different chapters (fruit and sweet pickles, sauerkraut, condiments, sauces, fermented drinks, and more). Brewing alcohol is also technically fermenting; however, the process is obviously different from fermenting vegetables, plus you will need some specialist equipment for brewing alcohol (fairly simple, inexpensive things, like a carboy, an airlock, an auto siphon, etc.), all of which will be covered in Chapter 10.

I'm a huge fan of kombucha, and I still remember the very first time that I made my own. It was so delicious, and I know it's so good for me. I do feel physically better when I drink it. I've never looked back, and it's something I regularly make now. You can find the recipe I use in Chapter 9—it is the very first recipe in that chapter. I have since learned about second fermentation, where you can add fruit, herbs, and spices, but when I first made it, I didn't know about that then. However, now a key favorite of mine is to add in lemon and ginger—it's so refreshing and delicious!

Key takeaways from this chapter:

1. Fermentation is where bacteria or yeast (sometimes fungi) convert sugars/starch into acid (bacteria) or alcohol (yeast) without oxygen (anaerobic reaction).

2. Fermented foods include things like sauerkraut, kimchi, tempeh, kombucha, kefir, yogurt, cheese, miso, natto, sourdough bread, salami, beer, and wine.

3. Fermented food contains probiotics (good bacteria) that aid digestion, help build your immune system, reduce heart disease, lower blood pressure, lower bad cholesterol (LDL) levels, and improve your mental health.

4. There are three types of fermentation: lactic acid fermentation, where sugar or starch is converted in lactic acid, alcoholic fermentation, where sugar or starch is converted into alcohol, and CO2, and acetic acid fermentation, where sugar or starch from grains or fruits is made into vinegar.

5. There are two stages of fermentation when making beer and wine: primary and secondary. Primary fermentation starts as soon as you add yeast to juice or wort. It is very busy, and there are visible bubbles. This usually takes 3–5 days. The secondary stage is slower and takes place over weeks—the yeast dies off due to rising alcohol content, and when the alcohol content reaches 12–15%, this will kill the yeast off, which prevents it from fermenting any further.

6. Pick vegetables that you and your family like to eat to ferment.

7. Some vegetables (red cabbage) will bleed the color into the brine. Vegetables may go quite dull during fermentation—this is natural.

8. Use fresh vegetables and filtered water for fermentation, measure and weigh ingredients, use pure salt, and use airtight containers. The ideal temperature for fermentation should be between 65 and 72°F (18–22°C), and the containers should be placed out of direct sunlight.

9. You can add herbs and spices to your fermentation recipes to give them a unique flavor.

10. You may need to use a weighing stone, a container, or a plastic bag filled with water to keep the vegetables submerged in brine.

11. If you don't have fermentation lids with airlocks, you will need to burp your jars by carefully unscrewing the lids but not opening them wide to let out the carbon dioxide but at the same time not let in lots of oxygen.

The next chapter will focus on quick pickles. You will find a good selection of delicious quick pickling recipes that are easy to follow and don't take a lot of time to make!

Chapter 3: Quick Pickles

This chapter is perfect for beginners to pickling. It contains recipes for quick pickles, which are exactly that. They don't take too long to make, and they give you delicious, preserved, tangy-tasting vegetables that you can start to eat with meals the very next day. Quick pickles are brined in a mixture of vinegar and salt, and the thinner you slice the vegetables, the quicker they will pickle. Some you can eat right away, and others are best left in the fridge overnight to be eaten the next day. The quick pickling method allows you to pickle a really wide variety of vegetables and fruits. Quick pickles don't keep as long as fermented pickles and usually need to be refrigerated.

To make quick pickles, you just need to make up a brine that typically contains water, vinegar, salt, and sometimes sugar. You can also add spices to it. Essentially, what you need to do is bring the brine to a boil, pour this over your jar of vegetables, allow it to cool, seal the jar, and refrigerate it, usually overnight.

Quick Pickling Recipes

1. Balsamic Vinegar Grapes

This is a lovely quick pickle recipe that makes grapes have a wonderful tang. They are perfect to accompany a charcuterie board or to garnish a cocktail. This should only take you 5 minutes to prepare.

Ingredients

- 1 cup (240 g) seedless red grapes
- 2 tablespoons filtered water
- ⅓ cup (80 ml) white balsamic vinegar
- ⅛ teaspoon pickling, pure, sea, or kosher salt
- 1 tablespoon granulated sugar
- ½ teaspoon black peppercorns
- 1 bay leaf
- ½ sprig rosemary

Instructions

1. Put the grapes in a jar with a sealed lid
2. Put the vinegar, water, sugar, peppercorns, bay leaf, rosemary, and salt in a saucepan on medium heat. Bring the liquid and spices to a boil, then reduce the heat for 2 minutes.
3. Let the liquid cool, then pour it over the grapes in the glass jar. Cover the jar with a lid.
4. Refrigerate the jar overnight and serve the next day. These will be fine in the fridge for 3–5 days, but if any remain after this time, then you should compost them.

2. Pickled Red Onions

This recipe is so quick—it will only take you about 2 minutes to prepare. Pickled red onions are delicious and are a perfect accompaniment with cheese on toast, sandwiches, tacos, and many other foods. Once you have pickled them, you can actually eat them within 2 hours if you needed to.

Ingredients

- 1 red onion, thinly sliced
- ⅔ cup (160 ml) white, wine, or cider vinegar

- ¾ cup (180 ml) filtered water
- 1 teaspoon pickling, pure, sea, or kosher salt
- 2 teaspoons sugar
- If you want to give more flavor to the recipe, you could optionally add fresh rosemary, thyme, dill, whole peppercorns, garlic, or chili.

Instructions

1. In a bowl, mix the vinegar, water, sugar, and salt. Keep mixing until the sugar and salt have dissolved.
2. Place the sliced red onions in a glass jar.
3. Pour the vinegar mixture over the onions. Seal the jar.
4. Let it stand at room temperature for at least 2 hours, then refrigerate for up to 2 weeks.

3. Pickled Green Beans

This recipe will give you lovely, crispy pickled green beans with a wonderful dill flavor. This recipe is from my grandma, and I still make it exactly like she did.

Ingredients

- 7 oz (200 g) green beans
- 1½ cups (360 ml) white vinegar
- 1 cup (200 g) granulated sugar
- 3 sprigs fresh dill

Instructions

1. Put green beans in a saucepan with salted water, and boil them for 4 minutes. Drain them, and put them into ice water until completely cold. Dry the green beans, then place in a glass jar along with the 3 sprigs of dill.
2. In another saucepan, put the vinegar and sugar and boil on medium heat until the sugar has dissolved. This will usually take about 1 minute.
3. Let the liquid cool completely. Then pour it over the green beans in the glass jar. Put a lid on the jar and refrigerate overnight before serving.

4. Pickled Apples

If you have an apple tree in your garden or simply have an abundance of apples from a farmer's market, making pickled apples is so tasty and a lovely thing to add to pork dishes or to have with a salad or a charcuterie or cheese board. This recipe will take approximately 15 minutes to prepare.

Ingredients

- 1 lb (450 g) apples, cored (approximately 2 medium apples)
- ½ cup (120 ml) white wine vinegar
- ½ cup (120 ml) water

- ½ cup (170 g) honey

- 1 teaspoon pickling, pure, sea, or kosher salt

- 3 star anise

- 3 cardamom pods

- 2 cinnamon sticks

- 2 bay leaves

- 1 teaspoon whole allspice

- 1 teaspoon whole peppercorns

Instructions

1. Cut your apples into thin slices using a mandoline. If you don't have a mandoline, you could use a peeler, or you could grate the apples to make a coleslaw effect. You can also cut them into thin batons.

2. Put the apple slices into a quart (0.95L) glass jar.

3. In a pan, boil the vinegar, water, honey, salt, star anise, cardamom, cinnamon, allspice, peppercorns, and bay leaves. Let the liquid cool.

4. Pour the brine over the apple slices.

5. Cover with a lid, then place in the fridge overnight. They should last in the fridge for up to 2 weeks.

5. Pickled Bell Peppers

In this recipe, it's entirely your call whether you decide to pick red, yellow, green, or orange bell peppers, or a mixture to pickle. It's a great way to use up home-grown peppers from your garden—they're nice to add to salads. This recipe should take around 20 minutes to prepare.

Ingredients

- 6 peppers in total (pick what colors appeal to you), julienned (cut into long, thin slices)

- 1 large red onion, thinly sliced

- 1 cup (240 ml) cider vinegar

- ⅓ cup (80 ml) water

- 1 cup (200 g) sugar

- 2 teaspoons pickling spice

- ½ teaspoon celery seed

Instructions

1. Put the peppers and onion in a glass bowl.

2. Wrap the pickling spice in double thickness of cheesecloth and tie with a string.

3. In a saucepan, put the vinegar, water, sugar and spice bag. Bring to a boil and boil for approximately 1 minute.

4. Put the pickling spice bag into the glass bowl with the peppers. Pour the cooled liquid over the top, and place in the fridge for 24 hours.

5. The next day, get rid of the spice bag, and place your peppers, onion, and brine into mason jars and seal with a lid. They can be kept for up to a month in the fridge.

6. Pickled Carrots with Daikon

This recipe should take no more than 20 minutes to prepare. It makes a lovely accompaniment to roasted meats, and it's nice on top of burgers or sandwiches.

Ingredients

- 1 cup (130 g) carrots, julienned (cut into long, thin slices)

- 1 daikon radish, peeled and julienned
- 2 jalapeno peppers, seeded and thinly sliced
- ¾ cup (180 ml) white vinegar
- ¾ cup (180 ml) water
- 1 teaspoon pickling, pure, sea, or kosher salt
- ⅓ cup (67 g) sugar
- 2 drops liquid smoke (optional)

Instructions

1. In a glass jar, place the carrots, radish, and peppers.

2. In a saucepan, heat the vinegar, water, salt, sugar, and liquid smoke until it comes to a boil. Simmer until the sugar and salt have dissolved. Let this cool.

3. Pour the liquid over the carrots and radish in the glass jar. Cover with a lid.

4. Ensure it has been refrigerated for at least 2 hours before eating. It can be kept in the fridge for up to 2 weeks.

7. Spicy Pickled Grapes

These make a lovely accompaniment to salads, cheese boards, or to garnish a cocktail. They should take around 20 minutes to make, which includes preparation and cooking time.

Ingredients

- 1½ lb (680 g) red seedless grapes, cut in half
- 1½ lb (680 g) green grapes, cut in half

- 1 banana pepper, sliced
- 2 jalapeno peppers, sliced
- 1 red chili pepper, sliced
- ½ cup (120 ml) white vinegar
- ½ cup (120 ml) cider vinegar
- ½ cup (100 g) sugar
- 4 drops hot pepper sauce
- 1 tablespoon coriander seed
- 1 teaspoon whole allspice
- 2 inches (5 cm) fresh ginger, peeled and finely sliced
- 4 cinnamon sticks

Instructions

1. Put both vinegars, peppers, sugar, cinnamon, ginger, coriander, allspice, and 4 drops of hot pepper sauce in a saucepan over medium heat, bring it to a boil, then let it simmer until the sugar has dissolved—this will take between 3 and 5 minutes.

2. Let the liquid cool.

3. Put your grapes in a jar and pour over the cooled pickling liquid.

4. Place in the fridge overnight before serving.

8. Mixed Vegetable Pickles

This can work particularly well if you grow your own vegetables. It allows you to pick the vegetables you like and pickle them together in a combined jar. This recipe takes about 10 minutes to prepare and 15 minutes in total.

Ingredients

The vegetables can vary depending on what you like, have grown, or have available at the time of year.

- 1½ cups (150 g) cauliflower florets

- 1 carrot
- 1 celery stalk
- ¼ cup (45 g) peppers
- 1 cup (240 ml) white wine vinegar
- ½ cup (120 ml) filtered water
- 2 teaspoons salt
- 2 tablespoons granulated sugar
- 4 teaspoons pickling spice
- 2 fresh bay leaves

Instructions

1. Wash the vegetables thoroughly to ensure there is no soil or bugs on them.
2. Cut the vegetables into bite-sized pieces.
3. Put the vegetables in a glass jar.
4. Place the vinegar, water, salt, sugar, pickling spices, and bay leaves in a saucepan, and bring the liquid to a boil for 3 minutes.
5. Let the liquid cool entirely, then pour it over the vegetables in the jar.
6. Put the lid on, and refrigerate it overnight before serving.

9. Pickled Rhubarb

Rhubarb has quite a natural tang of its own, but usually we associate it as something sweet. However, pickling rhubarb allows it to make a great savory accompaniment to cheese boards or salads. Pickled rhubarb is a lovely accompaniment to roasted chicken or fish too. This recipe should take 15 minutes in total.

Ingredients

- 14 oz (400g) rhubarb, cut into diagonal chunks ¼ to ½ inch (0.6–1.2 cm) thick
- 2 cups (480 ml) cider vinegar
- 1½ cups (300 g) sugar
- 1 tablespoon pickling, pure, sea, or kosher salt
- ½ cup (50 g) pickling spice
- 1 inch (2.5 cm) piece of fresh finger, peeled and sliced thinly

Instructions

1. Place in a saucepan the vinegar, sugar, salt, ginger, and spices. Ensure that the sugar has dissolved. Strain the liquid, and dispose of the solids.
2. Place the rhubarb in jars, and leave ½ inch (1.2 cm) of space under the lid. Pour the hot liquid into the jars, firmly place the lids on, and leave at room temperature overnight. The next day, place in the fridge. They will keep for up to a month in the fridge.

10. Pickled Green Cherry Tomatoes

If you grow your own tomatoes and have a lot of green tomatoes that you aren't sure what to do with, they make an incredible pickle. Once pickled, they make a great accompaniment to pastrami or corned beef sandwiches. You can put them on a skewer above a Bloody Mary cocktail or just eat them from the jar as a snack. This recipe should take approximately 10 minutes.

Ingredients

- 4 cups (600 g) green cherry tomatoes
- 2 red chiles
- ¾ cup (180 ml) white vinegar
- ¾ cup (180 ml) filtered water
- 2 tablespoons pickling, pure, sea, or kosher salt
- 1 tablespoon granulated sugar
- 1 clove garlic

Instructions

1. Put the cherry tomatoes in a glass container along with the clove of garlic and 2 chiles.
2. In a saucepan, heat the vinegar, filtered water, salt, and sugar until the salt has dissolved.
3. Let the liquid cool, then pour over the tomatoes, garlic, and chiles. Place the lid on the jar.
4. Let this stand for 2 hours, and then put the jar in the fridge, where it will be fine for up to 1 month.

11. Pickled Beets

Pickled beets are really easy to make, and we always pickle some when we have a bumper crop of fresh beets. This recipe should take 1 hour and 15 minutes in total (1 hour of this is cooking the beets).

Ingredients

- 10.5 oz (300g) beets (try to ensure that the beets are all similar in size)
- ⅓ cup (80 ml) malt vinegar
- ⅓ cup (80 ml) water
- ¼ teaspoon salt
- ⅓ cup (67 g) light soft brown sugar to give a more caramelized flavor

Instructions

1. Wash the beets with a toothbrush, and trim the stems.
2. Place the beets in a pan of cold water and bring to a boil, then simmer for 1 hour.
3. Once the beets are cooked and cooled, peel the skins and slice finely (using a mandoline if you have one available).
4. Put the slices of beets in a glass jar.
5. In a saucepan, combine the vinegar, water, sugar, and salt, and boil until the sugar has dissolved.
6. Pour the brine over the sliced beets, and let them cool to room temperature. Put a lid on.
7. Refrigerate the jar for at least an hour before serving. Pickled beets can last for up to 6 weeks in the fridge.

12. Pickled Prawns and Silverskin Onions

This recipe should take 10 minutes of preparation time and 15 minutes in total. If you are a fan of seafood and enjoy crunchy little onions, this will be a delight.

Ingredients

- 8 oz (230g) large prawns, cooked and peeled
- 8 silverskin onions
- ½ cup (120 ml) white wine vinegar
- ½ cup (120 ml) water
- 1½ tablespoons pickling spice
- 3 tablespoons granulated sugar
- ½ lemon

Instructions

1. Put the silverskin onions in a saucepan, cover them with water, and boil them for approximately 5 minutes until they feel tender. Drain them.

2. In a saucepan, put the water, vinegar, and sugar. Boil until the sugar has dissolved—this will usually take around 2 minutes. Let the liquid cool completely.

3. Place the cooked prawns, onions, pickling spices, and half a lemon in a glass container. Pour the cooled pickling liquid over the top. Cover with a lid. Place in a refrigerator overnight before serving. They will typically last for 3 days in the fridge.

13. Pickled Rainbow Swiss Chard Stalks

This is a lovely recipe that really gets the most out of your food and avoids food waste. Often, the stalks of chard are cut off because they're tough, and we tend to just eat the leaves. But having the stalks pickled makes a fantastic snack, and they can also be added to salads, eggs, or any dish that wants a sour accompaniment. This recipe should take 10 minutes to prepare and 15 minutes in total.

Ingredients

- 2 large bunches rainbow Swiss chard
- 1 small onion, sliced

- 1 cup (240 ml) cider vinegar
- ⅓ cup (80 ml) water
- 1 cup (200 g) sugar
- 2 teaspoons pickling spice
- ½ teaspoon mustard seed
- ½ teaspoon celery seed

Instructions

1. Take the leaves off the chard and put in the fridge to use with another meal.

2. Cut the stems into 2-inch (5 cm) pieces.

3. Put the stems in a jar along with the onion, pickling spice, celery seed, and mustard seed.

4. Place the vinegar, water, and sugar in a saucepan, and boil it until the sugar has dissolved.

5. Allow the mixture to cool before pouring over the chard stems and onion.

6. Cover the jar with a lid, and refrigerate it overnight before serving.

14. Pickled Garlic Mushrooms

Pickled mushrooms are super easy to make, and my friends always ask me to bring some to holiday gatherings, BBQs, picnics, and so on. They make a lovely accompaniment to charcuterie boards and work great as a steak topper too. This recipe should take 10 minutes to prepare.

Ingredients

- 1 lb (450 g) small button mushrooms
- 1 onion, cut into slices
- 4 cloves garlic, cut into slices
- ⅔ cup (160 ml) white wine vinegar
- ½ cup (120 ml) vegetable oil
- 2 tablespoons water
- 1 teaspoon salt
- ½ teaspoon pepper
- A few drops hot pepper sauce

Instructions

1. Put the vinegar, oil, water, salt, pepper, and hot pepper sauce in a jar, then add in the mushrooms, onion, and garlic.
2. Put the lid on the jar, and shake it gently, ensuring that all the mushrooms are covered.
3. Put the jar in the fridge overnight.
4. The next day, drain the liquid off before serving.

15. Pickled Baby Cucumbers

These are perfect in a salad or with a cheese board. They should only take 5 minutes to prepare and 10 minutes in total.

Ingredients

- 2 cups (300 g) baby cucumbers (These are a special type of miniature cucumber—they are about 2 inches (5 cm) long and have a crunchier texture than larger cucumbers. If you can't find baby cucumbers, you can use small Persian cucumbers, pickling Kirby cucumbers, English cucumbers, or even cucamelons instead.)
- 1 cup (240 ml) white vinegar
- ½ cup (5 g) fresh dill
- ¼ cup (50 g) sugar
- 1 teaspoon salt

Instructions

1. Place the mini cucumbers and dill in a glass jar.
2. Place the vinegar, sugar, and salt in a saucepan. Heat until the liquid is boiling, which should take a couple of minutes. Let the liquid cool, then pour it over the mini cucumbers and dill.
3. Cover the jar with a lid, and ensure it is refrigerated for at least an hour before you serve them.

16. Pickled Jalapenos

Pickling jalapenos makes them slightly less hot because some of the heat from the peppers will go into the brine. When you pickle them, they still say nice and crunchy. If you really don't like a lot of heat from your peppers, you can remove the seeds because these are their hottest part. You could also rinse them under cold water prior to pickling to reduce the heat. It's a good idea to wear gloves when preparing jalapenos because the oil from them can be hot, and you don't want to touch your face or eyes after touching jalapenos with your hands. This recipe should take approximately 15 minutes.

Ingredients

- 1 lb (450 g) jalapeno peppers, cut into rings
- ⅔ cup (160 ml) white vinegar
- 1½ cups (360 ml) water
- 5 teaspoons pure salt
- 4 teaspoons pickling spice

- 5 cloves garlic
- 1 cup (9 g) fresh dill

Instructions

1. Put the slices of jalapenos into a quart (0.95 L) glass jar along with the dill and garlic.
2. In a saucepan, put the vinegar, salt, pickling spices, and water and simmer until the salt has dissolved.
3. Let the liquid cool, then pour over the peppers, garlic, and dill.
4. Put this in the fridge for 7 days before eating, and you can keep them for up to 1 month in the fridge.

17. Pickled Corn

If you grow your own corn or have access to lots of fresh corn from a farmer's market, this recipe will allow you to keep eating corn even when it has gone out of season. It should take approximately 15 minutes to make.

Ingredients

- 4 corns on the cob (without the outer husk)
- 1 cup (240 ml) white vinegar
- ½ cup (120 ml) water
- ½ cup (100 g) sugar
- 1 teaspoon salt

- ½ teaspoon black pepper
- ¼ teaspoon red pepper flakes
- 2 garlic cloves, cut into slices

Instructions

1. Cut the corn off the cobs and place in glass jars.
2. In a saucepan, pour in the vinegar, water, sugar, garlic, salt, pepper, and red pepper flakes. Bring the liquid to a boil, then simmer until the sugar has dissolved. This should take approximately 2 minutes.
3. Let the liquid cool, then pour it over the corn. Put lids on the jars, and ensure they've been in the fridge for 2 hours before you serve them. The corn will last for up to 2 months in the fridge.

18. Pickled Cabbage

Both green and red cabbage can be pickled. It can make a lovely accompaniment to burgers or hot dogs. It can also add a nice balance to sweeter food—for example, if you have pulled pork, this can make a good accompaniment. The recipe takes around 10 minutes to prepare.

Ingredients

- 2½ cups (225 g) shredded cabbage
- 1 stick celery, cut into small chunks
- ½ green pepper, diced
- ½ cup (120 ml) vinegar
- ¾ cup (150 g) sugar
- ½ teaspoon salt
- ¼ teaspoon pepper
- ½ teaspoon celery seed

Instructions

This is a very simple recipe—you simply need to put all the ingredients in a bowl together. Ensure that the cabbage is covered, then cover the bowl, and place it in the refrigerator for at least an hour before serving. It will keep in the fridge for up to 2 weeks.

19. Pickled Strawberries

These make a delicious accompaniment to cheese. You could serve them on a toothpick or as part of a relish tray. The recipe should take 10 minutes to prepare.

Ingredients

- 2 lb (900 g) strawberries, hulled
- 1 green onion, finely chopped
- ½ cup (120 ml) rice vinegar (you can use white wine vinegar or champagne vinegar instead)
- 1 teaspoon sesame oil
- 1 teaspoon chili garlic sauce
- ½ teaspoon black sesame seed
- ½ teaspoon grated orange zest

Instructions

1. Place all the ingredients in a large bowl, and ensure the strawberries have been fully covered with the liquid.
2. Cover the bowl, and place in the fridge for at least an hour before serving.
3. You can place them in jars, sealed with a lid, and they will keep for up to 2 days in the fridge. They do taste best fresh because they can start to break down and become mushy with time.

20. Pickled Brussels Sprouts

Brussels sprouts seem to be as divisive as Marmite, but I love them! I love Marmite too, actually. Brussels sprouts can be roasted, grilled, steamed, boiled, or eaten raw. They're incredible pickled, especially with some onion, garlic, and chili. The recipe should take around 40 minutes in total to prepare and process.

Ingredients

- 3 lb (1350 g) fresh Brussels sprouts, trimmed and cut in half
- 1 onion, thinly sliced
- 1 sweet red pepper, finely chopped
- 2½ cups (360 ml) water
- 2½ cups (360 ml) white vinegar
- 3 tablespoons pure salt
- ½ cup (100 g) sugar
- 6 cloves garlic, cut in half
- 2 teaspoons red pepper flakes
- 1 tablespoon whole peppercorns
- 1 tablespoon celery seed

Instructions

1. Use a saucepan or a Dutch oven, and fill it ¾ full of water. Bring it to a boil. Place the Brussels sprouts into the water in batches, and cook them uncovered for 4 minutes. Remove with a slotted spoon, and place them in ice water. Drain them, and pat them dry.
2. Put the Brussels sprouts into 6 pint (473 ml) jars, and spread the garlic and pepper flakes among them.
3. In a clean saucepan, put in all the other ingredients, and bring them to a boil. Ladle the hot liquid over the Brussels sprouts, ensuring you leave at least ½ inch (1.2 cm) of space at the top of the jar. Ensure there are no air bubbles. Wipe the rims, and put the lids on firmly.
4. Next, place the jars into a canner with simmering water, and ensure the cans are completely covered

with water. Bring them to a boil for 10 minutes. Take the jars out, and let them cool.

I remember making my first jars of pickled mini cucumbers with my grandmother. I remember the sharp smell of vinegar, the light scent of dill, and putting in salt and sugar. I helped pour the vinegar, sugar, and salt into the saucepan, but because I was a little kid, my grandma heated it on the stove until it boiled. She let it cool, and then I poured it over the cucumbers and dill. I helped label the jars with their name and date. I recall us eating them the next day. Sometime later that night, she would make us pickled cucumber sandwiches for supper, on white bread, with butter, and the crusts cut off.

Key takeaways from this chapter:

1. Quick pickles are exactly that—quick. Some quick pickles take just 10 minutes to make, and some you can eat after a couple of hours in the fridge or by the next day.

2. Quick pickles tend to need to be refrigerated, and depending on what you've pickled, they may last from a few days to a few months.

3. Quick pickles brine is usually made from vinegar, water, salt, herbs, and sometimes sugar.

4. Quick pickles are great for cheese boards, charcuterie boards, as a cocktail garnish, with cheese toasties, with burgers, sausages, tacos, with chicken or fish, with pork dishes, as well as salads, among other things.

5. There's a wide variety of food you can pickle, from vegetables, like cucumbers, peppers, green beans, beets, onions, Swiss chard, carrots, green tomatoes, mushrooms, jalapenos, corn, cabbage, and Brussels sprouts, to fruits, such as grapes, apples, rhubarb, and strawberries.

6. Pickling can be great to use parts of vegetables and fruits that are usually not eaten, such as the stalks of rainbow chard and watermelon rind. This can help avoid food waste.

7. There are a number of spices and ingredients that are good to have prior to pickling. You don't want to put all of them in every pickle, but follow the recipe and tweak flavors accordingly. Things like pure salt, sugar, garlic, dill, ginger, onions, lemons, red pepper flakes, mustard seed, celery, chili, whole peppercorns, hot pepper sauce, orange zest, and pickling spices.

8. White vinegar is the most common type of vinegar to use when pickling, but you can purchase other vinegars, such as cider vinegar, white wine vinegar, champagne vinegar, and rice wine vinegar, and try them out with different foods.

The next chapter will focus on fermented pickles. The chapter starts with a quick recap on fermented pickles, then includes a nice selection of fermented pickle recipes. Sauerkraut and other cabbage recipes are not included in this chapter because Chapter 6 is dedicated to them.

Chapter 4: Fermented Pickles

When people hear of fermentation, many of them think of fermentation with alcohol, and while this is, of course, a thing (see the final chapter of this book), you can ferment a great many things, including vegetables, fruits, dairy, and meat! Fermentation allows you to preserve produce and has so many health benefits for your gut and to aid digestion. For people who have a homestead, fermentation is ideal because they get to preserve the food they've harvested, and it can last them throughout winter. Common fermented foods include sauerkraut, kimchi, yogurt, and sourdough bread, which are all achieved via lacto-fermentation.

When you ferment pickles, they are cured for a few weeks, then fermentation occurs, and the bacteria produce acids that preserve the food. They also create a distinctive fermented flavor. Sometimes, acid can be added after fermentation.

In lacto-fermentation, the *Lactobacillus* bacteria convert sugars into lactic acid to preserve the food and stop harmful bacteria from growing. Vegetables sit in a solution, and the sugars in the vegetables break down, while beneficial bacteria start to grow. Lactic acid is formed, and this preserves the food. By doing this, it can increase the vitamins and enzyme levels in the fermented vegetables and add probiotics, which keep our digestive system healthy. It is essential to ensure that there is enough acidity in your pickling liquid to prevent *Clostridium botulinum,* which can cause botulism.

Important Dos and Don'ts of Fermented Pickling

If you're following a recipe, ensure that you stick to the proportions of salt, water, and produce exactly. The salt will stop bad bacteria from growing and help the good bacteria to create lactic acid, which preserves the product. Ensure that you follow the guidelines on temperature and time during fermentation. The temperature is especially important during fermentation to ensure the acid levels are correct.

Ensure that you ferment cucumbers within 24 hours of them being picked. Never use produce that has any mold on it. Make sure that the produce you use is free of insects. If the produce is brown or dry, don't use it.

The salt you use is vital to stop bad bacteria from growing. It's important to use pure salt without any additives, such as iodine or anti-caking agents. You can use pickling, pure, kosher, or sea salt—I personally prefer using sea salt for fermenting. Never use less salt or more water than the recipe suggests.

Don't use hard water. If your water is hard, boil it for 15 minutes, and leave it for 24 hours before using. Ensure you remove both scum from the top and pour the water through a sieve to remove any sediment from the bottom. Ensure that your vinegar is 5% acidity (50-grain). If you don't know what acidity vinegar has, don't use it. Use fresh spices for best flavor.

Wash all fermentation equipment that you'll use in hot soapy water, and rinse it in very hot water before use. When you heat the liquid to pickle, ensure you don't use metal pans because these can give your pickles a funny color or add chemicals to your pickles, which you don't want. Use scales, cups, and spoons to ensure you measure out the correct quantities of things.

You will need a clean 1-gallon (3.8L) container for every 5 lb (2.3 kg) of vegetables that you intend to pickle. You can use food grade plastic or glass containers if you don't have a stone crock. If you have a 5-gallon (19L) stone crock, then you can use this to ferment 25 lb (11.3 kg) of vegetables.

You will need to keep the produce under the brine while it ferments. You can put a dinner plate or a glass pie plate inside the fermentation container to weigh down the produce. If you need to weigh it down further, you could put some sealed quart (0.95L) jars filled with water on top of the plate. Another option is to fill a food grade plastic bag with water and use this to weigh the plate down. You can also ensure the container is covered with a clean, heavy towel, which would prevent any insects or mold affecting the product.

Kahm Yeast

Sometimes kahm yeast can form at the top of your fermenting jars, and it's important not to confuse this with mold because it won't harm you or your fermented produce. On the right is a picture of what kahm yeast looks like.

This is an aerobic yeast that forms when all the sugars have been used up from the produce and the pH drops due to lactic acid forming. Some vegetables are more likely to have this kahm yeast, and it's typically sweeter vegetables, like carrots, peppers, and beets. It won't impact the taste of your produce at all. You can skim off as much as you can, but you're unlikely to get it all. Kahm yeast is white or cream in color and may have some air bubbles. Mold is fuzzy and can be white, black, pink, green, or blue. If your mold is any color other than white, throw the entire jar away. If you keep getting kahm yeast on your fermented products, you could try adding more salt to your brine or fermenting at a slightly lower temperature.[1]

Making Your Own Whey

A lot of fermentation recipes require whey. It's not too difficult to find and relatively inexpensive to buy, but you can make your own if you like. To make your own whey, put a container of plain whole yogurt into a dishtowel. Tie it on a cupboard door, and let it drip

[1] Image from https://www.fermentingforfoodies.com/kahm-yeast-mold/

into a jar. The liquid that's dripped off is probiotic-rich whey. The leftover yogurt in the towel is essentially the equivalent of Greek yogurt or cream cheese. If you can't use whey and need your recipes to be dairy free, you can replace it with kombucha or water kefir.

Fermented Pickles Recipes

This chapter does not include sauerkraut and other cabbage recipes because Chapter 6 focuses on this in great detail.

1. Fermented Dill Pickles

Ingredients

- 4 lb (1.8 kg) 4-inch (10 cm) cucumbers
- 2 tablespoon dill seed or 4 heads fresh dill weed
- ¼ cup (60 ml) 5% vinegar
- ½ cup (140 g) pickling, pure, kosher, or sea salt
- 8 cups (1.92L) water
- You can optionally add in 2 garlic cloves, 2 teaspoons pickling spice, and 2 dried red peppers

Instructions

1. Wash the cucumbers.
2. Cut 1/16 inch (1.5 mm) off the blossom end of each cucumber.
3. Leave ¼ inch (6 mm) of stem attached.
4. Put half the dill and half the spices at the bottom of your pickling jars.
5. Add in the cucumbers.
6. Put in the remaining half of your dill and spices.
7. In a saucepan, heat the vinegar, water, and salt.
8. Pour the pickling liquid over the cucumbers.
9. Weigh down the cucumbers, and put a lid on the jar.
10. Store at a temperature between 70 and 75°F (21–24°C) for 3–4 weeks while it is fermenting. If you don't have this temperature, produce can ferment between 55 and 65°F (13–18°C), but then it would take 5–6 weeks to ferment. Don't ferment in temperatures above 80°F (27°C) because the produce will become too soft.
11. Remember to burp your jars daily if you don't have fermentation lids with airlocks.
12. Check your container twice a week, and remove any scum or mold off the surface of the container. If the pickles look soft or slimy or smell unpleasant, then you need to throw them out immediately.
13. Once they have fermented, they can be kept for 4–6 months in the fridge—make sure to remove surface scum and mold if you see any.
14. If you wish to can your fermented pickles, then you need to pour the brine into a pan, heat it until it boils, then simmer it for 5 minutes. Pass this brine through coffee filters to make it clear. Then put the pickles into the jar, pour over the hot brine, leave ½ inch (1.2 cm) of headspace, adjust the lid, and process the jars in a hot water bath or a canner. You can put the jars into a hot water bath or a canner that has been filled halfway up with warm (120–140°F or 49–82°C) water, then ensure that hot water is added until it is an inch (2.5 cm) above the jars. The water should be heated until it

is 180–185°F (82–85°C), and this needs to be done for 30 minutes. You can check with a candy/sugar thermometer that the temperature of the water is correct throughout the entire 30 minutes. It doesn't need to be hotter than this, or else your pickles may go soft.

2. Fermented Cherry Tomatoes

I adore tomatoes, and we grow many different varieties, and a lot of them. We eat them with most meals. Because we grow a lot, sometimes more than we can use in salads, sauces, lasagnas, and so on, another way to make good use of our produce is to ferment our cherry tomatoes. We ferment them using a salt brine, and they are delicious!

When you ferment cherry tomatoes, it is best to use tomatoes that are not fully ripe because ripe cherry tomatoes are quite sweet, and you don't want to make tomato wine, as the sugars will be converted into alcohol. If the tomatoes are red, it's fine, provided they're quite firm. They go nicely on an appetizer platter or if you just want a fizzy snack.

Ingredients

- 4 cups (600 g) underripe cherry tomatoes
- 4 cups (960 ml) filtered water
- 3 tablespoons pickling, pure, kosher, or sea salt
- 2 stems fresh basil
- 4 cloves garlic
- 1 sprig fresh parsley
- ¼ teaspoon mustard seed
- ¼ teaspoon black peppercorns
- ¼ teaspoon coriander seed

Instructions

1. Place the peppercorns, coriander seed, and mustard seed into a quart (0.95L) jar.

2. Next, fill the jar with your cherry tomatoes, basil, garlic, and parsley.

3. Mix the water and salt to create a brine.

4. Pour the brine over the tomatoes, ensuring they are covered.

5. Use a weight to weigh the tomatoes down so that they are submerged and under the brine at all times.

6. Next, cover the jar with a towel.

7. Ferment the cherry tomatoes somewhere cool and dark for 8 days. A kitchen cupboard or a pantry would be ideal.

8. The tomatoes will have an almost effervescent, fizzy sparkling taste once they have fermented. After fermentation, you can put a lid on the jar and refrigerate for a further 2 weeks before eating. Some tomatoes may burst during fermentation, but this isn't an issue. They will keep for around 6 months in the fridge.

3. Fermented Baby Bok Choy

Bok choy is a wonderful thing to ferment. There are various flavors you can add depending on your taste preferences, but we love basil and lemon, spicy red pepper, garlic, and sesame.

Ingredients

- 14 oz (400 g) bok choy
- ¼ cup (22 g) cabbage leaves, sliced
- 1⅔ cups (400 ml) filtered water
- 4 teaspoons pickling, pure, kosher, or sea salt
- 2 slices lemon
- 1 teaspoon dried basil

Instructions

1. Ensure that you pick the freshest bok choy to ferment. It should have firm and crisp leaves that audibly snap. The bottom of the bok choy leaves should be white, and their tops should have a nice, bright green color. If the bok choy is limp or yellowing, then don't use it. Keep the bok choy in the fridge in a bowl of cold filtered water prior to fermenting it.

2. You can chop the bok choy, or if the leaves will fit in the jar, leave them whole.

3. Dissolve the salt in the water to make brine.

4. Put the bok choy and lemon slices into a mason jar, and pour over the brine.

5. Place a fermentation weight in the jar to weigh down the bok choy. Cover the jar with a lid.

6. The jar of bok choy will change as it ferments. After 48 hours, all the bok choy should be below the brine. Up to 10 days, there may be lots of bubbles produced. Between 10 and 14 days, the ferment may become cloudy, and it will smell sour. Between 14 and 21 days, the microbial population will be mostly *Lactobacillus*, and the bok choy will smell sour and will be preserved well. Smell and taste the bok choy after this time over 7 days, and when you find a smell and taste that appeals to you, then refrigerate it.

7. Remember to burp the jar daily while it's fermenting if you don't have a fermentation lid with an airlock.

8. Trust your taste. It should taste nice and sour. If it doesn't taste nice or tastes alcoholic, don't eat it.

9. After fermentation, bok choy should be placed in the fridge and should be consumed within 6 months.

4. Lacto-Fermented Radishes

Lacto-fermentation is a good method to preserve radishes. It's quick and easy, and they make a nice, healthy snack. Because lacto-fermented radishes are milder than raw radishes, even children may like the taste of these. They remain crunchy, which is a lovely texture. Fermented radishes make a great snack instead of crisps or cookies. They can also be added to salads and go nicely with beets, eggs, tuna, celery, chicken, and feta. They also make a nice accompaniment to sandwiches, burgers, pulled pork, stuffed peppers, and other dishes.

Ingredients

- Radishes (typically 2 bunches will fill a quart (0.95L) jar). The color and size of the radishes does not matter.

- Non-chlorinated water and non-iodized salt (pickling, pure, kosher, or sea salt). Use 1.5 tablespoons of salt for every 2 cups (480 ml) of water.

- Optional herbs/spices—you can add a couple of cloves of crushed garlic, dill, thyme, sage, hot peppers, pickling spice, mustard seeds, chili flakes, or whole peppercorns.

- You can optionally add ½ cup (120 ml) of vinegar to this recipe if you choose to do so (but it's not necessary).

Instructions

1. Wash the radishes in cold water, and remove the greens. Use as many as needed to fill a jar.

2. Place the sliced radishes in a clean, sterilized jar.

3. Add any herbs or spices you want to include.

4. Add the salt to water, and stir it to help it dissolve. There needs to be enough brine to cover all the radishes.

5. Pour over the brine, and ensure that the radishes are submerged. You can wight them with a fermentation weight or small glass jars filled with water. The radishes need to remain under the brine at all times.

6. Once you have the radishes weighted under the brine and a bit of space at the top of the jar, put the lid on tightly. You may see bubbles appear in the jar. Remember to burp the jar daily if you don't have a fermentation lid with an airlock.

7. It's sensible to stand the jar of fermented radishes in a bowl, or if you have lots of jars, on a baking tray because throughout the fermentation process, some brine may bubble up out of the jar and spill, and you don't want to create a mess or stain any kitchen work surfaces. The jar should be kept at room temperature while it's fermenting. If the jar looks foggy, this is just part of the process, don't worry. It will take approximately 1 week to ferment your radishes, and when the jar clears, usually the fermentation process is done. It may never be quite as clear as the liquid you initially put in the jar, but it will be less cloudy.

8. After fermentation, you can leave the glass weight in the jar, and you can store your fermented radishes somewhere cold, like a fridge or a root cellar.

9. Do ensure that you use a clean fork each time you remove radishes from the jar.

10. If you want to, you can add other vegetables in to ferment with your radishes, such as peppers, turnips, cabbage, carrots, or cauliflower. The recipe and process remain the same.

5. Spicy Fermented Carrots

Fermented carrot sticks are a delicious, healthy snack for the family. They're great to put in lunch boxes for kids and adults alike, and they are easy to make. In the summer, when we have plenty of fresh carrots, we use them to snack on, but during the winter, these fermented carrot sticks are perfect.

Fermented carrots are a fabulous way to ensure your family gets lots of good, healthy probiotics in their gut too. Fermenting helps carrots release beta-carotene, which the body then converts into vitamin A, and this helps you to have good eye health, a strong immune system, and healthy skin. When you decide to ferment carrots, you get to choose what flavors you select to go with them. Some options could include dill, garlic, and pickling spice. You can also mix carrots with beets for a sweeter taste.

Ingredients

- 4–6 large carrots, cut into sticks
- 1 onion, sliced
- 1 jalapeno pepper
- 2 cups (480 ml) non-chlorinated water
- 3 teaspoons pickling, pure, kosher, or sea salt

Instructions

1. Mix the salt and water to make the brine.
2. Wash and cut the carrots into sticks.
3. Place the carrots into a quart (0.95L) jar, leaving 1 inch (2.5 cm) of headspace.
4. Add the sliced onion and jalapeno pepper.
5. Cover the carrots with the brine. If needed, use a weight to keep them submerged.
6. Put a lid on the jar, and remember to burp it daily if you don't have a fermentation lid with an airlock.
7. Put the carrots into a dark place (ideally a kitchen cupboard) for a week to allow them to ferment.
8. After this, store them in the fridge—they will keep there up to a month.

6. Fermented Brussels Sprouts with Garlic and Ginger

These sprouts are full of probiotics, and they are a wonderful accompaniment for many different diets, including paleo, keto, and vegan or plant-based diets. They are packed full of flavor and give a good boost to the immune system with garlic and ginger.

Ingredients

- 2 lb (900 g) Brussels sprouts, cut in half
- 4 cups (960 ml) warm water
- 4 tablespoons pickling, pure, kosher, or sea salt
- 1 bulb garlic (with approximately 15 cloves)
- 2 inches (5 cm) fresh ginger, cut into thin slices

Instructions

1. Mix together the water and salt until the salt has dissolved.
2. Put the Brussels sprouts, garlic, and ginger in glass jars.
3. Pour the brine over the Brussels sprouts, garlic, and ginger. Ensure that the water covers them and there is a 1-inch (2.5 cm) gap at the top of the jar.

Make sure to keep the produce submerged in the brine.

4. Seal the lid, and leave the jars in a warm location for 14 days. You can check on them every couple of days to ensure that the vegetables stay under the brine. Remember to burp the jars daily if you don't have fermentation lids with airlocks.

5. After this time, the Brussels sprouts should taste sharp and vinegary.

6. Place them in the fridge—they will keep there for up to 6 months.

7. Fermented Green Tomatoes

If you grow your own tomatoes, sometimes you'll get green tomatoes that don't ripen before the plant is past its best. While you can try to ripen green tomatoes indoors, or you can have fried green tomatoes, another option is to make delicious fermented green tomatoes. The recipe should take approximately 10 minutes to prepare.

Ingredients

*   Green tomatoes, enough to fill a quart (0.95L) jar

*   Non-chlorinated water

*   2 tablespoons whey or ½ tsp culture starter (this is optional, you don't have to use this)

*   1 tablespoon pickling, pure, kosher, or sea salt

*   4 cloves garlic

*   3 sprigs fresh dill

*   1 tablespoon peppercorns

Instructions

1. Chop your tomatoes into equal sized chunks. If you have smaller tomatoes, you can leave them whole.

2. Place them into a quart (0.95L) jar along with the herbs and whey or culture starter if you're using this.

3. Add the water, leaving 1 inch (2.5 cm) of space at the top of the jar.

4. Add the salt, fasten the lid, and shake the jar so that the salt dissolves.

5. Undo the lid, and use a weight to weigh the tomatoes down so that they stay under the brine.

6. Cover the jar with a towel and a rubber band. If you have a fermenting crock, you could use that, but it's not required if you're new to fermenting and don't want to rush out to buy a whole new lot of equipment just yet. Leave them to ferment at room temperature for 7 days. They will be similar to dill pickles but more tart.

8. Fermented Garlic

I adore garlic, and I think it's a wonderful addition to many meals. It is so flavorsome and really adds some oomph to a lot of dishes. When you lacto-ferment garlic, it will mellow the raw garlic taste, which can sometimes be overwhelming. It will allow you to get the best from the enzymes and nutrients in the garlic, and when you eat it, it tastes like a lovely mix between raw garlic and roasted garlic. Fermented garlic is very easy to make and will improve your gut flora. It is best to use lacto-fermented garlic in recipes where you don't need to cook it because if you cooked it, the heat would likely destroy all the good probiotics that you've created from fermenting. So, it's best used in recipes like garlic salad dressing, pesto, garlic butter, dips, fermented garlic paste, or salads (for example, Caprese salad).

Ingredients

- 10 heads garlic
- 4 cups (960 ml) water
- 2 tablespoons pickling, pure, kosher, or sea salt

Instructions

1. Peel the garlic.
2. Place the cloves of garlic into mason jars.
3. Mix the salt and water until the salt has dissolved.
4. Don't fill the garlic and brine all the way to the top of the jar, and ensure your brine is just covering the garlic.
5. If you want to speed up the fermentation process, you can add a teaspoon of organic apple cider vinegar or sauerkraut juice.
6. Ensure the garlic is always under the brine so that it doesn't go moldy.
7. If you want to add any optional flavors, such as pickling spice or herbs, like oregano or basil, you can do so.
8. Cover the jar with a lid, and remember to burp the jar daily if you don't have a fermentation lid with an airlock.
9. You can store the jar at room temperature in a cupboard or somewhere dark.
10. Keep the garlic fermenting for 3–4 weeks until there are no more fermentation bubbles.
11. If the garlic has a green/blue color after fermentation, this is natural, and it is still safe to eat.
12. When fermentation has finished, you can place the jar in the fridge. It will keep there for up to 2 months.

9. Fermented Jalapenos

These fermented jalapenos are a perfect accompaniment to things like tacos, nachos, enchiladas, or sandwiches. They also go nicely with salads or breakfast eggs. You can also make use of the brine that contains a good kick of heat after you've eaten the peppers by adding it to soups, salsas, and sauces. Like with all fermented recipes, they contain great probiotics and antioxidants that have many health benefits, including boosting your immune system and being great for gut health.

In the past, we found that our pepper plants produced so many peppers at once that we didn't know how to use them all up, and fermenting is a great way to preserve them. When you ferment them, they remain firm and have a tangy, spicy, delicious taste. This recipe could not be simpler—it literally has just three ingredients! The taste is incredible and guaranteed to bring some spicy heat to dishes.

Ingredients

- 2 cups (180 g) jalapeno peppers, sliced—ensure you pick peppers that are as fresh as possible, with smooth skin and no dents or blemishes. If you haven't grown the peppers yourself but have bought them, buy ones that are not bagged because bagged peppers are often triple washed and won't have the natural microbes found on vegetables. If you can only buy bagged, then you could add a tablespoon of sauerkraut juice or another ferment to start the fermentation process.

- 3 cups (720 ml) warm water

- 3 tablespoons pickling, pure, kosher, or sea salt

- Jalapenos are perfectly fine to be fermented with just these ingredients, but if you want, you can add fresh garlic or bay leaves too.

Instructions

1. Chop the jalapenos into circles about ¼ inch (6 mm) thick, discard the stem, and you can leave the pith and seeds if you want extra heat.

2. Place the chopped jalapeno peppers in glass jars.

3. In a saucepan, boil the water, let it cool a little, and then dissolve the salt into it.

4. If you wish to add garlic or bay leaves to your jars, you can do so.

5. Pour the brine over the jalapenos, and weigh them down so that they are fully submerged under the brine. Cover the jar with a lid.

6. After a couple of days, you may see bubbles appearing, and you'll need to burp the jar daily if you don't have a fermentation lid with an airlock.

7. Jalapenos should be fermented between 2 and 5 weeks. Once the brine is mostly clear, the fermentation process has finished. You can place them in the fridge, and they will keep there for up to 6 months.

10. Fermented Asparagus

Asparagus is so delicious in many different meals. By fermenting it, this means that you have asparagus on hand all throughout the year and not just in the spring when it's seasonal. Fermented asparagus makes a great snack that's filled with wonderful, healthy probiotics. It has a salty taste, some sourness from the fermentation, and it's delicious. Asparagus itself is full of great nutrients, such as antioxidants (purple asparagus contains more than green). If you're growing it yourself, you will need to be patient, because it will take 3-4 years to grow, but it will give you approximately 1.5 lb (680 g) of asparagus per plant, and the plants will last for decades. For fermented asparagus, you can use pretty much the same brine that you would use to pickle cucumbers. This recipe should take 10 minutes in total to make, and that includes 5 minutes of preparation time.

Ingredients

- 1 bunch asparagus (with the woody ends cut off)

- 2 cups (480 ml) warm water

- 2 tablespoons pickling, pure, kosher, or sea salt

- 3 cloves garlic, crushed
- 1 tablespoon fresh dill
- 2 teaspoons mustard seeds
- ½ teaspoon red pepper flakes

Instructions

1. Dissolve the salt in warm water to create a brine to use later.

2. Place the crushed garlic, mustard seeds, red pepper flakes, and dill at the bottom of a jar.

3. Next, pack in the asparagus into the jar as tightly as you can.

4. Pour the brine over the asparagus and spices, ensuring you leave 1 inch (2.5 cm) of space at the top of the jar. Ensure the asparagus is all submerged below the brine, using a pickling weight, a glass jar, or a food safe plastic bag filled with water.

5. Seal the jar with a lid, and leave it at room temperature for 3 weeks. If you live in a warm place, the fermentation will occur quicker than somewhere cold. Remember to burp the jar daily if you don't have a fermentation lid with an airlock.

6. You can keep the jar in the fridge after fermentation. It will keep up to 6 months there.

11. Fermented Zucchini

Zucchini have *Lactobacillus plantarum* bacteria on their surface, which can mean that they ferment faster than other vegetables. Zucchini generally need to be fermented for 2 weeks, but if you want it to have an extra sour flavor, you can ferment them for up to 4 weeks. As with all other fermented vegetables, they are very good for gut health. The recipe below is one of my favorites—it's light, fresh, and zingy, with zucchini fermented along with thyme, lemon, and red pepper. Zucchini fermentation is similar to cucumber fermentation. Zucchini contain water, fiber, and minerals, which can help reduce inflammation. When zucchini are fermented, they produce GABA (Gamma-amino-butyric acid), which can help relieve anxiety, improve mood, inhibit cancer cells, reduce PMS, help with ADHD, is good for building lean muscle, can stabilize blood pressure, and relieve muscle pain. Zucchini are naturally soft and spongey, so do not expect this recipe to give you something that has a crisp pickle texture.

Ingredients

- 14 oz (400 g) zucchini
- 1⅔ cups (400 ml) filtered water
- 2 tablespoons pickling, pure, kosher, or sea salt
- 1 slice lemon
- 1 sprig thyme
- 1 teaspoon red pepper flakes

Instructions

1. Ensure that the zucchini you select to ferment are fresh, firm, and hydrated. They should feel hollower than a cucumber when you tap them. Ensure that they don't have any mold or soft spots on their skin and no indentations or black marks.

Smaller zucchini are better to ferment than large ones. The larger a zucchini is, the soggier it will be. The zucchini you select should be a rich green color. If you can buy organic, this is best so that the bacteria have not been killed off by chemical pesticides.

2. Wash the zucchini in cold water.

3. Chop the zucchini up into pieces that work for you. It could be spears, chips, spirals, or shredded with a grater. It depends on what texture you want it to be.

4. Dissolve the salt in the water to make a brine.

5. Fill mason jars with your zucchini.

6. Add in the lemon, thyme, and red pepper flakes (or any other herbs/spices you want to use). You could put in bay leaves, green tea leaves, or grape leaves to give you slightly firmer fermented zucchini.

7. Pour over the brine, ensuring the zucchini are fully covered. Remember to leave an inch (2.5 cm) of headspace. Place a weight on top to keep them submerged below the brine. Firmly put the lid on and leave to ferment for 2 weeks. Remember to burp the jar daily if you don't have a fermentation lid with an airlock.

8. You can taste test the zucchini after 2 weeks and see how it tastes for you. If you want it to have a tangier sour taste, then you can let it ferment for 2 more weeks.

9. When the jar of zucchinis tastes how you want it to, then you can place it in the fridge.

12. Fermented Giardiniera

Giardiniera is an Italian pickle, and it uses vegetables that would have otherwise been preserved in oil or vinegar. Instead, this recipe uses fermentation as a preservation technique. If you want to make it spicy, you can add chili peppers. It's an attractive-looking pickle with a fabulous taste. It's something that you may find your family snack on, or you could serve it with a cheese board. You could also include it as a sandwich filling or serve it with BBQ food to accompany hot dogs or hamburgers. It can make a great topping for pasta, and it can be put on pizzas. You can use it in salads too.

It's the vegetables themselves that provide the culture for fermentation, so it's best to pick fresh, organic vegetables if you can for this recipe. If you grow your own vegetables, this is a great way to preserve your summer harvest. Other vegetables you can add to the recipe are radishes and green beans. If you want to reduce the salt to teaspoons per jar, you can, but then you would need to use a starter, like cultured apple cider vinegar or fermented vegetable brine.

Ingredients

- 1 small cauliflower (approximately 3 cups or 300 g)

- 2 sweet peppers

- 2 carrots

- 1 onion

- 2 stalks celery
- 2–4 hot peppers (optional, if you want to make it spicy)
- 3 cloves garlic
- 2 bay leaves
- 2 sprigs thyme
- 3 cups (720 ml) filtered water
- 2 tablespoons pickling, pure, kosher, or sea salt

Instructions

1. Wash the vegetables.
2. Prepare your vegetables by chopping the cauliflower into bite-sized pieces. Thinly slice the peppers, carrots, onion, and peel and cut the garlic cloves into halves. Dice the celery stalks.
3. Pack the vegetables into jars.
4. Dissolve the salt in the water and pour over the vegetables in the jars. Remember to leave an inch (2.5 cm) of headspace. Ensure the vegetables are fully submerged below the brine (use a weight).
5. Place the jars in a dark location to ferment (a kitchen cupboard is ideal) for 3–7 days. Remember to burp the jars daily if you don't have fermentation lids with airlocks. Then you can store the jars in your fridge for up to 6 months.

13. Fermented Rainbow Chard

If you have grown a lot of chard, you may typically eat the leaves but be at a bit of a loss with what to do with the stalks. Rather than have food waste, it's a great idea to lacto-ferment them. This recipe includes some garlic, and the chard itself has lots of vitamins and minerals that are more easily absorbed by your body due to the fermentation process.

Ingredients

- 10–12 stalks rainbow chard
- ½ onion
- 4–6 cloves garlic
- Filtered water
- 1 teaspoon pickling, pure, kosher, or sea salt
- Pinch loose black tea leaves (optional)

Instructions

1. Wash the chard, and cut the stalks into pieces.
2. Pack the stalks tightly in a glass jar.
3. Put the onion and garlic into the jar.
4. Sprinkle in the salt (1 tablespoon of salt per quart (0.95L) of water). If you decide to use the black tea, add that too. It won't change the taste of the chard, but it will keep it crisper.
5. Pour the brine over everything in your jar, leaving 1 inch (2.5 cm) of space at the top.
6. Put an airtight lid on the jar. Leave it in a dark, cool place to ferment for 3 days, then put it in the fridge. Remember to burp the jar daily if you don't have a fermentation lid with an airlock.

14. Fermented Red Onions

These fermented red onions are quick and easy to do. They ferment in 2 weeks, and they are so versatile and can be used in a lot of different recipes. You can use them on sandwiches, hot dogs, or burgers as well as in wraps and salads. You can have them with potatoes or macaroni as well as at a picnic or a potluck. You can add them to coleslaw or potato salad, have them with tacos, put them on pulled pork or grilled cheese sandwiches, and much more—they really liven up a meal and make it delicious!

Ingredients

- 2 large red onions, sliced

- 2 cups (480 ml) water

- 2 tablespoons pickling, pure, kosher, or sea salt

- You may decide to add black peppercorns, bay leaf, or rosemary if you like

Instructions

1. Slice the onions, and place them in a jar. If you wish to add in the optional black peppercorns, bay leaf, or rosemary, then you can do so.

2. Dissolve the salt in the water to make a brine.

3. Pour the brine into the jar over the onions (and spices if you've used them). Ensure there is 1 inch (2.5 cm) of space at the top of the jar.

4. Close the jar with an airtight lid, and put it somewhere out of direct sunlight to ferment for 2 weeks. Remember to burp the jar daily if you don't have a fermentation lid with an airlock.

5. After this time, store the jar in the fridge.

15. Fermented Daikon Radish Spears

Daikon radishes become nice and sour when they've been fermented, but they still retain their crunch. If you like spicy flavors, you could add in some red pepper flakes or hot Korean chili paste. This is a recipe that ferments slowly in the fridge over months. You can even leave them for years if you like a really sour taste. They are great to accompany salads or as an appetizer. They also work well in cocktails. This recipe should take about 20 minutes to prepare.

Ingredients

- 1 lb (450 g) daikon radishes, cut into spears (approximately ½ inch (1.2 cm) thick and 3 inches (7.5 cm) long)

- 2 cups (480 ml) water

- 2 tablespoons pickling, pure, kosher, or sea salt

- 2 tablespoons red pepper powder or red pepper flakes—this is optional and will make the recipe spicy

Instructions

1. Scrub the daikon gently under running water to clean them. Clean it well, but don't scrub it to an immaculate finish because you want some of the good bacteria to remain for fermentation.

2. Cut the daikon into spears about ½ inch (1.2 cm) thick and 3 inches (7.5 cm) long.

3. Dissolve the salt in the water to make a brine.

4. Put the daikon spears in a glass jar, and if you're using red pepper flakes, add them too. Then pour over the brine, making sure the daikon is fully submerged (use a weight to keep them submerged). Leave 1 inch (2.5 cm) of space at the top of the jar. Seal the jar with an airtight lid.

5. You can leave it to ferment for 4 weeks, then place in the fridge. Remember to burp the jar daily while it's fermenting if you don't have a fermentation lid with an airlock. When it's in the fridge, it will still continue to ferment, but much more slowly.

16. Fermented Carolina Coleslaw

This coleslaw originates from the Southeastern United States. By fermenting the vegetables, this gives it a wonderful taste and makes the vegetables easier to digest. The dressing in the slaw is like a vinaigrette salad dressing, and it doesn't contain any mayonnaise. This is a nice slaw to go with fatty food, as it cuts through the fat cleanly and crisply with the sourness of the slaw.

Ingredients

- 1 lb (450 g) green cabbage
- ½ lb (225 g) celery
- 1 carrot
- 1 onion
- 1 green bell pepper
- ½ apple
- ⅓ inch (8 mm) ginger root
- 3 oz (90 ml) sesame, olive, or coconut oil
- ¼ cup (85 g) honey
- 4 teaspoons pickling, pure, kosher, or sea salt
- Black pepper to taste
- 2 teaspoons dry mustard

Instructions

1. Thinly slice or grate the cabbage, onion, and bell pepper. Grate or shred the apple, carrot, and celery. Place all the vegetables in jars.

2. Dissolve the salt in the water and pour over the vegetables, ensuring they're all covered in the brine. Seal the lid, and ferment them for 4–7 days. Remember to burp the jar daily if you don't have a fermentation lid with an airlock.

3. Drain the vegetables using a colander. Press them with your hands to get rid of the liquid (keep this to one side though).

4. Next, add ½ cup (120ml) of the liquid with the honey, oil, mustard, and ginger and mix well. Add the salt and pepper. If you want a sourer taste, then add some more of the liquid that you kept to one side. You can also save any liquid you have left to use as a starter to ferment something later. Or you can mix it with oil and spices to make a salad dressing. Some people also drink a little in the morning to aid their digestion.

17. Fermented Radish and Carrot Slaw

This is a Vietnamese inspired recipe, and it's a lovely slaw to keep in your fridge that can give your salads a nice, delicious flavor and color. It also contains plenty of beneficial bacteria that will improve your gut health. This recipe includes basil, mint, cilantro, and lime, which are added to shredded carrots and radishes. This slaw can be added to sandwiches, burgers, or a Buddha bowl. For good gut health, it's recommended to eat a variety of different fruit and vegetables, and this slaw can add seven vegetables to your meals with ease. Because the vegetables are fermented, they're easier to digest, and you'll gain more nutrients from them as well as probiotics. During the fermentation process, the radishes become less tangy, and you'll taste more of the herbs used.

Ingredients

- 1 lb (450 g) radishes, grated or sliced

- 1 lb (450 g) carrots, peeled and grated
- 1 tablespoon pickling, pure, kosher, or sea salt
- 1 lime, use the zest and the juice
- ¼ cup (7 g) fresh mint
- ¼ cup (5 g) fresh basil
- ¼ cup (4 g) fresh cilantro (coriander)
- 1 teaspoon coriander seed
- 1 tablespoon fish sauce (optional)

Instructions

1. Chiffonade (finely cut into long, thin strips) the herbs and mix with lime zest, juice, coriander seeds, and fish sauce if you decide to use it.
2. Grate the carrots, and slice or grate the radishes.
3. Add the carrots and radishes to the herb bowl.
4. Add 1 tablespoon of salt, ensuring it is mixed thoroughly into all the ingredients.
5. Place the ingredients in a glass jar, leaving a 1-inch (2.5 cm) gap at the top.
6. Fill the jar with water (remember to leave a 1-inch (2.5 cm) at the top).
7. Ensure you use a fermentation weight to weigh the ingredients down below the brine. Fasten the jar tightly with a lid.
8. Place the jar in a bowl in case any brine overflows. Keep the jar somewhere out of sunlight (like a kitchen cupboard) for 5–7 days. Remember to burp the jar daily if you don't have a fermentation lid with an airlock.
9. Next, place the jar in the fridge, and you can use it for 6–12 months.

Useful Tips

Get rid of any woody or brown bits on the radishes prior to fermenting them. To get more flavor out of the coriander seeds, crush them a little with the back of a spoon prior to using. While fish sauce may smell fishy in the bottle, it won't after fermentation, and it will really enhance the taste of your slaw. Fish sauce is usually made with anchovies and salt, and you'll find it as an ingredient in many sauces and dressings, like Caesar salad dressing, for example.

18. Fermented Pumpkin Spears with Cardamom

This recipe is a lovely way to preserve pumpkins. It will give you a firm pickled pumpkin that has an earthy flavor. You'll need a sharp knife to cut your pumpkins into spears. You could use your fermented pumpkin in pumpkin pies or hearty warming soups. Cardamom gives a lovely flavor to the pumpkin that is reminiscent of autumn. To successfully ferment pumpkin, it's important to reserve a bit of the rind because it's from this rind that the beneficial bacteria will ferment.

Ingredients

- Enough pumpkin slices to fill your jars
- A slither of pumpkin rind
- 2 teaspoons pickling, pure, kosher, or sea salt
- Water (distilled or filtered)
- 8 cardamom seeds (if you're not keen on cardamom, you can leave this out, or you could try cloves or cinnamon sticks)

Instructions

1. Prepare your pumpkin by peeling it and cleaning it out. Keep a slice of the rind because the bacteria on it will help your pumpkin to ferment.
2. Cut the pumpkin into spears that fit into jars, but leave 1 inch (2.5 cm) of headspace.

3. Pour water over the pumpkin, and add the salt and cardamom seeds. Ensure the pumpkin is fully submerged in brine.

4. Place a lid on the jar, and leave it to ferment at room temperature for 2–3 weeks. Remember to burp the jar daily if you don't have a fermentation lid with an airlock.

5. You can taste the pumpkin after 2–3 weeks to see if it has reached the desired level of tanginess. Then you can place it into a fridge to consume when convenient.

19. Fermented Dilly Beans

Green beans are one of my favorite vegetables to eat. I love their texture and bite. Having them fermented is wonderful—with the sour tang and the flavor of the dill and garlic, they make a lovely snack. You can use green, yellow, or purple beans, or a mixture to give a more colorful effect. Salty and crunchy, they make a perfect part of an appetizer. Fermenting is a great way to make use of your garden harvest, and they will fill you with healthy probiotics, giving you wonderful gut health.

Ingredients

- Enough green beans to fill a quart (0.95L) jar
- 1 small hot pepper (optional, depending on taste)
- 5 garlic cloves
- 2 flower heads dill (or 2 sprigs fresh dill and 1 tablespoon dill seed)
- 1 teaspoon mustard seed
- 1 teaspoon black peppercorns
- 2 bay leaves
- Pickling, pure, kosher, or sea salt
- Filtered water

Instructions

1. Put all the ingredients listed above in a jar.

2. Create a brine by mixing 1 tablespoon of salt for every 2 cups (480 ml) of water.

3. Pour the brine over the green bean mixture in the jar.

4. Ensure all the vegetables are covered in the brine, and weigh them down with a fermentation weight.

5. Cover the jar with a cheesecloth and a rubber band, and place it in a kitchen cupboard.

6. Taste the beans after a week to see if they appeal to you. If they feel too crunchy, you can let them ferment for another week. If your kitchen is very cold, it may take longer.

7. After this time, you can put a lid on the and keep it in the fridge—the beans will keep there for 2 months.

20. Fermented Sugar Snap Peas

These make a lovely, healthy snack. If you have them growing in your garden, it's great to make up a couple of jars of fermented sugar snap peas. You can use herbs that you grow yourself to add to the recipe—we use fresh basil and cilantro (coriander). These sugar snap peas are both crispy and spicy. They're a lovely snack on their own, and I love having them on a summer evening with a refreshing drink. You can also add them to salads or cut up into small pieces to make devilled eggs with.

Ingredients

- 2–3 cups (330–500 g) fresh sugar snap peas
- 2 cups (480 ml) distilled water
- 1 tablespoon pickling, pure, kosher, or sea salt

- Fresh herbs, such as dill, basil, cilantro, and rosemary
- 1 teaspoon red pepper flakes

Instructions

1. Mix the salt and water and stir until the salt has dissolved to make a brine.
2. Put the herbs of your choice at the bottom of the jars.
3. Pack your sugar snap peas into the jars, ensuring you leave 1½ inches (3.8 cm) of headspace.
4. Sprinkle ½ a teaspoon of red pepper flakes into each jar and some sprigs of fresh herbs.
5. Pour the brine over the sugar snap peas, ensuring they're fully submerged.
6. Use a glass weight to weigh down the peas and stop them from floating.
7. Put a lid on the jar and keep at room temperature for 3–7 days, then try them—they should be crispy, spicy, and snappy. Remember to burp the jar daily if you don't have a fermentation lid with an airlock.
8. When they have fermented to a level you're happy with, then you can place them in the fridge.

We get a lot of produce on our homestead, and try as we might to use it up and share it with family and friends, we still have excess produce at times, and making lacto-fermented pickles is a wonderful way for us to preserve to produce and have it throughout the year with dishes when it's no longer in season. We had an abundance of radishes this year, and lacto-fermenting them gives them a much milder taste, and we'll be able to have them for salads and sandwiches throughout the winter.

Key takeaways from this chapter:

1. Fermentation allows you to preserve harvested food that will last you through the winter.
2. Use recommended salt, water, and produce quantities in recipes, and do not change the proportions. Use pickling, pure, kosher, or sea salt and filtered water.
3. Keep produce under brine using glass weights or other methods discussed.
4. Kahm yeast is white and is not an issue. If you see any other color mold, though, do not eat the fermented produce and throw the jars out.
5. You can make whey by putting yogurt into a dishtowel and letting it drip. The dripped liquid is probiotic rich whey.
6. If you need a dairy-free version of whey, you can use water kefir or kombucha.
7. Fermenting can mellow the taste of some vegetables—it will make radishes milder and garlic less raw and strong, with a taste somewhere in between raw and roasted.
8. Making things like radish and carrot slaw is a great way to get yourself and your family to eat more vegetables—it's a really tasty accompaniment to a meal. Because it's fermented, it's easy to digest and full of good probiotics.

The next chapter will focus on fruit and sweet pickles, with 10 fruit pickle recipes and 6 sweet pickle recipes. You will learn easy, fail-safe tips to pickle apples, grapes, mango, carrots, cherry tomatoes, sweet onions, sweet beets, and more.

Chapter 5: Fruit and Sweet Pickles

This chapter covers both fruit and sweet pickles, really demonstrating the diversity of things you can pickle from fruit to salad ingredients. The fact that these pickles combine both the sourness of pickles with the sweetness of fruit or vegetables, like cherry tomatoes and carrots, which have their own natural sweetness, makes these truly delicious to eat, hitting so many flavor pairings at once.

Fruit Pickle Recipes

1. Fermented Cinnamon Apples

What a delicious fruit and spice combination to ferment! It will taste just like an apple pie and Christmas all mingled together. These are delicious with some yogurt for breakfast or on their own as a snack. You could also make apple pies out of them, or you could have them as a healthy dessert. They're fabulous with ice cream or on top of waffles as well. Full of probiotics, they are great for you, as well as super tasty! It's a simple recipe to follow, and the flavor is wonderful. The probiotics will help your immune system and give you healthy gut bacteria too.

Ingredients

- 3–4 cups (375–500 g) sweet apples, chopped with seeds removed
- 1 teaspoon pickling, pure, kosher, or sea salt
- Water (non-chlorinated)
- 2 tablespoons fermented tea from a SCOBY (symbiotic culture of bacteria and yeast) or some whey
- Juice from 1 lemon (not from concentrate)
- 1 tablespoon ground cinnamon

Instructions

1. Use a SCOBY—if you don't have one, you can use whey. Mix this with the salt, cinnamon, and lemon juice.
2. Place apple wedges (or chopped pieces of apple to make them fit better) in a bowl. Coat them in the mix of SCOBY, salt, cinnamon, and lemon juice.
3. Place the coated apples in glass jars, and then fill them with non-chlorinated water. Ensure you leave 1 inch (2.5 cm) of headspace.
4. Put the lid on and keep at room temperature and out of direct sunlight for 2 days.
5. After 2 days, refrigerate the apples. You can keep them in the fridge for up to 3 months.

2. Fermented Berries

Making fermented berries is a great way to use up excess fruit. It is important to stop the fermentation after 2 days by refrigerating them because otherwise it would start turning into alcohol. When berries are fermented, they're will give you excellent probiotics. They're easy to digest, and they will boost your immune system too. Berries are an excellent source of antioxidants, which help reduce inflammation and can protect against ageing and disease. They regulate hormones, prevent infections, and help balance pH levels. Fermented berries are delicious on top of yogurt, in smoothies, with ice cream, on top of baked goods, or to accompany desserts. You can use any berries except strawberries to ferment because strawberries are too acidic for lacto-fermentation.

any longer than this because the berries have a high sugar content, and they will turn into alcohol.

6. Next, place the jar in the fridge, and use the berries within 1–2 months.

3. Pickled Red Grapes

These pickled red grapes make a perfect accompaniment to cheese or pate. They also go perfectly on salads, and they're nice as a healthy snack too.

Ingredients

- 1lb (450 g) red grapes
- 1 cup (240 ml) apple cider vinegar
- ¼ cup (60 ml) water
- 1 cup (200 g) granulated white sugar
- ¼ teaspoon black peppercorns
- ¼ teaspoon cloves
- ⅛ teaspoon yellow mustard seed
- ½ vanilla bean
- 1 cinnamon stick

Instructions

1. Rinse the grapes, and take off the stems.
2. Cut the end of the grape that had the stem.
3. Place the vinegar, water, and sugar in a saucepan, and bring it to a boil.
4. Put the grapes in a jar, and pour the hot brine over them.
5. Let them cool, place a lid on the jar, then put it in the fridge.
6. Leave them in the fridge for 24 hours before consuming.

4. Pickled Sliced Mango

If you have lots of mangoes, it can be a great idea to pickle them, and this recipe contains a lovely Asian flavor too.

Ingredients

- 2 cups (380 g) any berries except strawberries
- 2 tablespoons sugar (organic cane sugar and palm sugar work best, but you can also use the same amount (2 tablespoons) of raw honey or Grade A Dark-Robust or Grade A Very Dark-Strong (formerly Grade B) maple syrup)
- ½ teaspoon culture starter or 2 tablespoons whey
- ¼ teaspoon pickling, pure, kosher, or sea salt
- Filtered water

Instructions

1. Place your berries in a jar.
2. Mix the culture starter or whey with 2 tablespoons of water, sugar, and salt.
3. Pour the mixture over the berries, ensuring you leave 1.5 inches (3.8 cm) at the top of the jar.
4. Keep the berries under the brine by weighing them down.
5. Put a lid on the jar and keep at room temperature for 2 days. Don't leave at room temperature for

Ingredients

- 7 mangoes

- 3 cups (720 ml) water

- 1 tablespoon vinegar

- ¼ cup (70 g) pickling, pure, kosher, or sea salt

- 1¼ cups (250 g) white sugar

Instructions

1. Peel and slice the mangoes, and cut into pieces that are 1 inch (2.5 cm) thick.

2. Put the mango slices and 3 tablespoons of salt in a bowl.

3. Put the remaining salt, water, and sugar in a saucepan, and bring it to a boil.

4. Remove the saucepan from the heat, pour in the vinegar, and let it cool for 15 minutes.

5. Drain the salted mango slices, and place them in jars.

6. Cover the mango slices with the cooled brine. Seal, place in the fridge, and leave for around 2 days until the mangoes become very yellow.

5. Pickled Blueberries

This pickling recipe is quick and easy and can be adapted to virtually any fruit or vegetable. Blueberries have great health benefits for you because they're filled with antioxidants, so they can protect against ageing and cancer as well as exposure to things like pollution or cigarette smoke. Blueberries are full of vitamins C and K, manganese, and dietary fiber. They can also help manage cholesterol and blood sugar.

Ingredients

- Blueberries, enough to fill a jar

- 1 cup (240 ml) water

- 1 cup (240 ml) vinegar

- 1 tablespoon pickling, pure, kosher, or sea salt

- ½ cup (100 g) sugar

Instructions

1. Wash the blueberries.

2. Pack them into the jar.

3. Put the water, vinegar, salt, and sugar in a saucepan, and bring the brine to a boil. If you have a lot of jars, you can make more brine—just make sure to keep the proportions of water, vinegar, salt, and sugar the same.

4. Pour the brine over the fruit in the jars.

5. Seal the jars, and keep them in the fridge.

6. Use within 1–2 months.

6. Pickled Pears

Pickled pears are a nice accompaniment to meatloaf, and they also go nicely with soft cheeses, like Brie, Camembert, or goat cheese. They make a great Christmas gift, and if you have any Christmas cold cuts left over, they're really nice with that too. I adore the texture of pear, and I they are a great fruit to pickle.

Ingredients

- 4 lb (1.8 kg) small pears

- 4 cups (960 ml) cider or white wine vinegar

- 2 lb (900 g) caster sugar

- 1 lemon or orange

- 2 inches (5 cm) ginger root, sliced

- 2 cinnamon sticks

- 10 cloves

- 2 teaspoons black peppercorns, slightly crushed

- 1 teaspoon allspice berries, slightly crushed

Instructions

1. Zest the lemon or orange, and place the zest in a pan with the ginger, juice from the lemon or orange, vinegar, sugar, cloves, peppercorns, allspice berries, cinnamon sticks, and stir over a gentle heat until the sugar has dissolved.

2. Peel, core, and halve the pears, then place them in the pan, and simmer for 15 minutes until the pears are tender.

3. Take the pears out the pan with a slotted spoon, and put them in a colander to drain.

4. Boil the liquid for 15 minutes until it becomes like a syrup in consistency. The quantity of the liquid should reduce by approximately ⅓.

5. Put the pears in jars, then cover with the hot syrup. Cover the jars with lids, and store somewhere cool and dry for 1 month before consuming.

7. Pickled Cherries

The tartness of pickled cherries can go nicely with blue cheese, fig and ham, or with most cheeses and cheese boards. Some people also like to put a pickled cherry into cocktails, and they're great to use in salad dressings or when making chutneys.

Ingredients

- 1 lb (450 g) cherries

- ¾ cup (180 ml) cider vinegar

- ¾ cup (180 ml) water

- ½ cup (100 g) caster sugar

- 2 bay leaves

- 1 teaspoon chili flakes

- 2 teaspoons coriander seed

Instructions

1. Place the water, sugar, vinegar, coriander seeds, chili flakes, and bay leaves in a pan, and bring it to

a boil to dissolve the sugar. Simmer it for 5 minutes, then remove from heat.

2. Place the cherries in a jar, then pour over the hot brine. Seal the jar, and leave it for 2 weeks before consuming.

3. The cherries in this recipe did not have their stones removed, as they keep their shape better whole. You can remove the stones, of course, but if you decide not to remove them, you need to warn whoever is intending to eat the cherries so that they don't choke or break a tooth biting into a stone.

4. The jar can be stored in a cool, dry place for up to 1 year.

8. Quick-Pickled Plums

These pickled plums are delicious in a sandwich, or to accompany salads, or if pancakes are your thing, they go nicely on top of pancakes. Ensure the plums are ripe but firm to get the best effect. Even after you have eaten the plums, you can use the brine in salad dressings.

Ingredients

- 3 plums
- ¼ cup (60 ml) apple cider vinegar
- ¾ cup (180 ml) water
- 1½ teaspoons pickling, pure, kosher, or sea salt
- ¼ cup (50 g) granulated sugar
- 7 black peppercorns
- 1 star anise or 2 cloves

Instructions

1. Ensure the plums you pick are ripe but firm. Rinse them, then slice them into ½-inch-thick (1.2 cm) slices.

2. Put the plum slices in a jar.

3. In a saucepan, heat the vinegar, sugar, salt, star anise or cloves, and peppercorns. Bring the mixture to a boil, then pour this over the plums, ensuring they're completely submerged.

4. Let this cool for 20 minutes.

5. Place in the fridge overnight before eating.

6. The longer the plums are in the brine, the stronger they'll become.

7. You can keep them in the fridge for up to a month.

9. Pickled Nectarines

These pickled nectarines are very easy to make, and they're a delicious accompaniment to a cheese plate or a salad. They can make a nice addition to pork dishes too. They're delicious swirled into some yogurt for a delicious dessert.

Ingredients

- 6 nectarines
- 2 cups (480 ml) white vinegar
- 2 teaspoons pickling, pure, kosher, or sea salt
- ¾ cup (150 g) granulated sugar
- ¾ teaspoon black peppercorns
- ¼ teaspoon red pepper flakes
- 3 star anise
- 1 bay leaf
- 1 cinnamon stick

Instructions

1. If you're using a canner, prepare it, and place 3 lids in a saucepan with water to simmer.

2. Prepare 3 jars.

3. Rinse the nectarines, and slice each nectarine into approximately 12 pieces.

4. Place the water, white vinegar, sugar, and salt into a pan. Bring the liquid to a boil.

5. Divide the spices between the 3 jars you are using.

6. Once the brine is boiling, add the nectarines into it and stir, then take the pan off the heat.

7. Ladle the fruit into the jars—you can use a wooden skewer or a chopstick to help the nectarine slices settle into place.

8. Pour the brine over the nectarines, ensuring they are fully submerged and there are no air bubbles.

9. Put the lids on the jars, and if you're processing them, place the jars into a boiling water bath and process for 10 minutes.

10. After processing, let them cool, check the seals, and wash any stickiness off the jars.

11. If you're not processing the jars but simply storing them in the fridge, then you need to allow them to sit in the brine for at least 48 hours before consuming.

10. Pickled Watermelon Rind

Watermelon rind slices have a delicious sweet and sour tang of sugar and vinegar, combined with warm spices of ginger, cinnamon, and cloves. They make an excellent appetizer, or they can be wrapped in bacon and served with creamy goat cheese. They are also perfect for BBQs and to accompany cheese boards. What's extra great about this recipe is that it's reducing food waste and using bits of the watermelon that most people usually throw away.

Ingredients

- Rind from a watermelon, approximately 1½ lb (680 g)
- 1–2 green chilies, thinly sliced
- Filtered water
- 1¼ cup (300 ml) white wine vinegar
- 4 tablespoons pickling, pure, kosher, or sea salt
- 1½ cups (300 g) raw cane sugar
- 1 cinnamon stick
- ¼ cup (25 g) ginger, thinly sliced
- 2 teaspoons black peppercorns

Instructions

1. When you cut up your watermelon, leave a thin layer of the pink/red watermelon flesh on the rind.

2. Next, use a vegetable peeler to peel off the outer green skin. Then slice the rind into ½-inch-thick (1.2 cm) strips.

3. Fill a pan with 2 quarts (1.9L) of water, and add in 4 tablespoons of salt. Add the rind, and bring it to a boil, then reduce the heat and simmer for 5 minutes. Strain the rind through a colander, but make sure to collect the brine.

4. Pour 3 cups (720 ml) of the brine back into the pan, and add in the white wine vinegar and raw cane sugar. Add the peppercorns, cinnamon stick, and ginger. Bring this to a boil until the sugar has dissolved. Next, add the watermelon rind back in, and simmer it for 10 minutes.

5. Remove the pan from the heat, and allow it to cool for 30 minutes.

6. Use tongs to lift the watermelon rind out of the brine, and place the rinds into sterilized jars. Add the sliced chilies, ginger, and cinnamon sticks to the jars.

7. Pour enough brine over the rind to ensure it is fully submerged, let the jars cool fully, and then store the jars in the fridge.

8. You can start eating them the next day, but it's best if you leave them to pickle for 3 days. They will keep for about a month in the fridge.

Sweet Pickle Recipes

1. Sweet Pickled Cucumbers

If you have homegrown cucumbers, and more than you know what to do with, this is a great recipe to preserve them, keeping them crunchy and sweet. They can be either a delicious snack or a refreshing accompaniment to meats and cheeses.

Ingredients

- 9 pickling cucumbers
- 1 large sweet onion, thinly sliced
- Crushed ice
- 1 cup (240 ml) white vinegar
- ½ cup (120 ml) cider vinegar
- 1 cup (240 ml) water
- ¼ cup (70 g) pickling, pure, kosher, or sea salt

- 1 cup (200 g) sugar
- 12 cloves garlic, crushed
- 2 tablespoons mustard seeds
- 1 teaspoon celery seed
- 4 bay leaves
- ½ teaspoon whole peppercorns

Instructions

1. Slice the cucumbers, and put them in a bowl with the onions and salt. Put crushed ice over them. Leave them for 3 hours, then drain well.

2. In a large saucepan, place the sugar, water, vinegar, mustard seed, celery seed, peppercorns, and bring it to a boil. Add the cucumbers and simmer for 5 minutes.

3. Place the contents in jars, leaving ½ inch (1.2 cm) of headspace. In each jar, place 3 crushed garlic cloves and a bay leaf.

4. Put the lids on the jars. Place the jars into a canner with simmering water, ensure they're completely submerged, and keep them bubbling away for 10 minutes. Remove the jars, and let them cool down.

2. Sweet Pickled Carrots

These carrots retain a nice crunch to them. They're really good and tangy. They are ideal for buffets, to accompany salads, in packed lunches, and as a healthy treat to accompany a sandwich.

Ingredients

- 1 lb (450 g) carrots
- ⅔ cup (160 ml) white vinegar
- ¾ cup (180 ml) water
- ¾ cup (150 g) sugar
- 3 whole cloves
- 1 tablespoon mustard seed

Instructions

1. Julienne (cut into long, thin strips) your carrots into 3-inch (7.5 cm) strips. Add 1 inch (2.5 cm) of water to a saucepan, and put your carrots in there and bring to a boil. Turn down the heat and simmer for 4 minutes. Drain and rinse the carrots in cold water. Put them in a bowl and place to one side.

2. In a different saucepan, combine the water, sugar, cloves, vinegar, and mustard seed. Bring to a boil, then reduce heat and simmer for 10 minutes. Let the liquid cool.

3. Place the carrots in a jar. Pour the brine over the carrots.

4. Place in a fridge for at least 8 hours overnight. After this time, discard the cloves and cinnamon. These will keep in the fridge for around 3 months.

3. Sweet Pickled Cherry Tomatoes

We get hundreds of cherry tomatoes each year, and our vegetable garden is currently swarming with tomato plants, so we'll have a great harvest again. We love tomatoes, and they're so versatile with a wide range of recipes, sauces (one of my favorites is marinara), chutneys, salsas and so on. But we get so many tomatoes we have to preserve them to use throughout the rest of the year. This recipe is ideal for that.

Ingredients

- 8 cups (1.2 kg) cherry tomatoes
- 4 cups (960 ml) champagne vinegar (or you can use apple cider vinegar)
- 1¼ cups (300 ml) water
- 1 tablespoon pickling, pure, kosher, or sea salt
- ¾ cup (150 g) sugar
- 5 cloves garlic
- 5 teaspoons dill seeds (cumin is an alternative you could use if you like/prefer the taste)
- 10 sprigs dill

Instructions

1. Saute (fry quickly in a little hot oil) the dill seeds and peppercorns in a dry pan.

2. Put the toasted dill seeds and peppercorns into clean jars, approximately 1½ teaspoons per jar. Add 2 sprigs of dill and 1 garlic clove to each jar. Then pack the tomatoes into the jars.

3. In a saucepan, place the water, sugar, salt, and vinegar, and bring it to a boil. Pour this over the tomatoes, ensuring there is a ½-inch (1.2 cm) gap at the top of the jars. Ensure there are no air pockets. Put the lids on the jars.

4. Put your sealed jars into a canner, with enough water to cover the jars by an inch (2.5 cm), bring the water to a boil, and process the jars for 15 minutes. Turn off the heat. Leave the jars in the canner for

a few minutes, then remove from the water, and let them cool completely.

4. Pickled Sweet Onions

These recipe uses larger onions that are chopped up and pickled. They're a lovely thing to give as a Christmas gift to people and also make a fantastic accompaniment for BBQs because they work wonderfully well on top of burgers or hot dogs as a kind of relish.

Ingredients

- 8 cups (400 g) sweet onions
- 1¾ cups (400 ml) white vinegar
- 2 tablespoons pickling, pure, kosher, or sea salt
- 1 cup (200 g) sugar
- 1 teaspoon dried thyme

Instructions

1. Slice and chop the onions finely.
2. Put the onions into a colander, sprinkle the salt over them, and mix it all in. Let the onions stand in the salt for an hour before rinsing, draining, and squeezing them to get rid of excess liquid.
3. In a saucepan, put in the vinegar, sugar, and thyme, and bring it to a boil. Add the onions and bring to a boil again before reducing heat to simmer them for 10 minutes.
4. After that, put the onion mixture in jars, remembering to leave ½ inch (1.2 cm) of headspace.
5. Put the lids on the jars, and place them into a canner with simmering water. Ensure they are completely covered with water. Bring to a boil and keep them there for 10 minutes.
6. Remove jars carefully, and let them cool.

5. Sweet Pickled Garden Vegetables

I used to buy pickled vegetables in jars from the supermarket regularly, and my favorite item in those jars was pickled cauliflower. Now, we grow our own vegetables, and this recipe is perfect for preserving a mixture of our harvest into exciting and vibrant jars that make a lovely accompaniment to salads.

Ingredients

- 2 lb (900 g) assorted fresh vegetables. These can include Kirby cucumbers, carrots, celery, cauliflower, peppers, and pearl onions.
- ¼ cup (60 ml) cider vinegar
- 2½ cups (600 ml) water
- 1½ teaspoons pickling, pure, kosher, or sea salt
- ¼ cup (50 g) sugar
- 8 sprigs fresh dill
- 1 teaspoon pickling spice
- 1 teaspoon whole black peppercorn

Instructions

1. In a large glass bowl, place the water, vinegar, sugar, salt, pickling spice, and peppercorns and mix thoroughly.
2. Wash and dry your vegetables and cut into small pieces. Add the sprigs of dill, then pour the brine over them all.
3. Cover the bowl with plastic wrap, and refrigerate it for 3–4 days before serving. You could also place this into sealed jars and keep them in the fridge for up to a month.

6. Sweet Pickled Beets

If you've produced more beets than you can possibly manage to consume, then making sweet pickled beets is a fantastic way to preserve your harvest. Beets are highly nutritious and are packed with fiber, potassium, iron, manganese, vitamin C, and vitamin B9. Beets are popular with athletes because they can improve stamina and performance. They're good for lowering blood pressure and improving circulation. Pickled beets may help fight oral cancer cells and leukemia. Consuming pickled beets will help you to have healthy digestion and prevent inflammatory diseases. You could eat pickled beets as an accompaniment to pork chops, roast chicken, stir-fries, or even in sandwiches. You can also add it to coleslaw or have it with feta cheese, fresh greens, and prawns for a vibrant salad.

Ingredients

- 10 lb (4.5 kg) fresh small beets
- 1 quart (0.95L) vinegar
- 1 tablespoon pickling, pure, kosher, or sea salt
- 2 cups (400 g) sugar
- 2 tablespoons whole cloves
- 1 tablespoon allspice

Instructions

1. Place the beets in a pan of water, bring it to a boil, and boil them for about 40 minutes until they are tender (the larger the beets are, the more time it'll take).

2. Save 2 cups (480 ml) of the beet water for later—you can drain the rest.

3. After the beets have cooled, cut them into ½-inch (1.2 cm) pieces.

4. Boil the jars you intend to use for 10 minutes to ensure they're sterilized (remember to remove the rubber seals before sterilizing).

5. Place the beet pieces and whole cloves in the jars.

6. Place the 2 cups of beet water, plus the vinegar, sugar, salt, and allspice in a saucepan, bring it to a boil, then let it simmer for 5 minutes.

7. Pour the hot brine into the jars with the beets, ensuring you leave ½ inch (1.2 cm) of headspace.

8. Put the lids on the jars. Place them in a canner, add water, bring it to a boil, and ensure the jars are completely immersed in boiling water by at least an inch (2.5 cm). Process the jars for 10 minutes.

9. Using tongs, remove the jars, and let them cool for 24 hours.

10. Sealed jars can be stored in a cool, dry place for a year. Once you open a jar, then place it in the fridge, and use it within 6 weeks.

We have a lot of apple trees, and we're fortunate that they produce a lot of apples. We make apple pies, apple sauce, and apple juice, but one of our favorite things to do to preserve the apples is to make fermented cinnamon apples, and these are incredible for breakfast and also lovely as a dessert with some yogurt. You get the sharpness and tang from the apples, the warmth from the cinnamon spice, and the amazing probiotics, which are a great boost to the immune system.

Key takeaways from this chapter:

1. Remember that berries ferment quickly due to the natural sugars in them. You can put them in the fridge to stop the fermentation process and prevent them from becoming alcohol.

2. Remember you can sterilize jars by heating them in the oven for 10 minutes.

3. When pickling cherries, they keep their shape better if you keep the stone in. However, it is important to warn whoever is eating them that they

contain a stone, so that they don't choke or break a tooth.

4. When pickling fruits, after you've finished eating them, you can use the brine to make a salad dressing.

5. Pickling and fermentation can be a fantastic way to use up more parts of the fruit so that there is reduced food waste. An example of this is pickled watermelon rind.

The next chapter will focus on sauerkraut, kimchi, and other cabbage pickles. You will find tasty recipes to replicate German-inspired sauerkraut as well as delicious kimchi recipes that use carrot, radish, cucumber, and apples. You will also learn how to pickle a variety of different types of cabbage.

Chapter 6: Sauerkraut, Kimchi, and Other Cabbage Pickles

Sauerkraut is finely cut cabbage that has been fermented by lactic acid bacteria. Despite the German name (which translates to "sour cabbage"), it actually originated in China over 2,000 years ago. Nowadays, people all over the world eat sauerkraut. Kimchi is a traditional Korean dish consisting of salted and fermented vegetables, most commonly using napa cabbage or Korean radish. Sauerkraut has a milder taste than kimchi. Kimchi can often be spicy and have chili powder, chili paste, gochujang, garlic, vinegar, and salt. Both sauerkraut and kimchi are fermented and therefore contain excellent probiotics, giving you good bacteria to help you have a healthy gut. This chapter covers different types of sauerkraut and kimchi recipes, plus some other fermented and pickled cabbage recipes too.

Sauerkraut, Kimchi, and Other Cabbage Pickles Recipes

1. Sauerkraut

Sauerkraut is one of the easiest fermented dishes to make. It can be made using only 2 ingredients—cabbage and salt. The longer you let it ferment, the more distinctive the taste will be. You may have had more than your share of coleslaw. So, another option is to turn cabbage into sauerkraut, which is delicious to accompany sausages. It's very inexpensive to make, and it's a really healthy topping for sandwiches or a nice side dish for meals.

Ingredients

- 1 medium head green cabbage (approximately 2 lb or 900 g)

- 1 tablespoon pickling, pure, kosher, or sea salt

Instructions

1. Quarter the cabbage, and remove the core. Slice the cabbage, and put this in a large, shallow bowl.

2. Sprinkle the salt over the cabbage.

3. Knead the cabbage—this will help release the juices and will make your sauerkraut tangier. You can knead it by hand or use a potato masher. You should ideally do this for 10 minutes, and you should have got enough juice out of the cabbage to cover it.

4. Put the cabbage in jars, keep packing it down, and ensure it is covered by the brine (the liquid you squeezed out during kneading). Ensure that there is ½ inch (1.2 cm) of space at the top of the

container. Weight the cabbage down using either fermentation weights, a small glass jar filled with water, or a food safe plastic bag with water.

5. Let it ferment. You can use an airlock lid and fermentation weights. Other people just use butter muslin and a small jar to weigh down the cabbage under the liquid. If you have put a regular lid on, you'll need to open it a bit every few days to release the pressure. It will need to ferment for 2 weeks at room temperature (60–70°F or 15–21°C). You can taste it after this time and then place it in the fridge, where it will be fine for up to 6 months.

2. Beet and Cabbage Sauerkraut

This recipe is delicious, containing beets, cabbage, apple, ginger, and garlic. It's a lovely accompaniment to salads, and it's great on top of avocado on toast or as a side dish to meat or fish. The beets are earthy and sweet, the cabbage is crunchy, and the ginger gives it some heat. The apples are nice and sweet too. It's great to eat during the cold and flu season because it will give you immune boosting nutrients to fight germs, helped by the fact that it contains garlic and ginger too, as well as the probiotics from fermentation that keep your gut flora healthy. Beets are great to purify blood, stimulate your immune system, detoxify your body, and they have anti-inflammatory properties too.

Ingredients

- 2 medium raw beets
- 1 medium apple
- 1 small cabbage head
- 3 cloves garlic
- 1 inch (2.5 cm) ginger
- 2 tablespoons pickling, pure, kosher, or sea salt

Instructions

1. Wash the cabbage in cold running water, and ensure that you take off any outer leaves that look discolored. Wash and peel the beets, ginger, and garlic.

2. If you have one available, use a mandoline to slice the beets, apples, and shred the cabbage. If you don't have a mandoline, cut them using a knife.

3. Place the shredded cabbage in a bowl, and add the salt.

4. Massage the salt into the cabbage so that it breaks down and softens. This usually takes around 3 minutes. Then leave the cabbage in the salt for 10 minutes. It may release salty water.

5. Add in the beets into your cabbage/salt mixture. Leave for 2 minutes.

6. Next, mix in the apples, ginger, and garlic.

7. Place your vegetables and salt water mix in jars. The salt water mix from the cabbage should cover all your vegetables. You need to ensure there is at least a 1-inch (2.5 cm) gap at the top of the jar.

8. If there is not enough naturally released liquid from your salt and cabbage mix to cover the vegetables, then mix 1 teaspoon of salt with 1–1½ cups (240–360 ml) of water, and use that to top up the jars and ensure the vegetables are covered. You could use 1–2 cabbage leaves at the top of the jar to stop the contents from floating up and a glass weight to keep everything submerged under the brine.

9. Place the lids onto the jars, and place the jars on a plate (in case any liquid overflows so that it doesn't make a mess). Leave the jars on the kitchen counter or in a cupboard for 3–5 days. You will see tiny

bubbles in the jar that rise to the top, which shows that fermentation has started. Remember to burp the jar daily if you don't have a fermentation lid with an airlock. If any scum appears at the top of the jar, you can quickly remove this with a spoon.

10. After 5 days, place the jar in the fridge, which will slow down the fermentation process. After 5 more days in the fridge (10 days in total), you can start eating it if you choose to do so.

Useful Tips

- Wear gloves to avoid the beets staining your hands. If you do get beet juice on your skin, put lemon juice and salt on this before washing with soap and water, and this will help to remove the stains.

- While the sauerkraut may initially smell of garlic, once it has been placed in the fridge, you won't notice it at all.

3. Purple Sauerkraut

This is a nice variation of the traditional sauerkraut recipe using red cabbage, which results in purple sauerkraut. Not only does it look lovely, it also tastes delicious, and recently, it's become my "go-to" recipe when I crave some sauerkraut.

Ingredients

- 2 medium red cabbages
- 2 tablespoons pickling, pure, kosher, or sea salt
- ½ cup (120 ml) whey (optional)—it helps get a consistent result, and it allows you to use less salt because it's rich in lactic acid. If you don't want to use whey, double the salt.

Instructions

1. Gently wash the cabbage, but don't sterilize it. Remove the outer leaves.

2. Cut the cabbage up.

3. Mix it with the salt and optional whey.

4. Pound the cabbage and salt/whey mixture with a wooden spoon or mallet for 5–10 minutes to release juices.

5. The salt will stop the bad bacteria from forming until lactic acid is produced to preserve the food.

6. Put the cabbage in jars, and use a glass fermentation weight to keep the cabbage submerged under the brine. Cover the jars with lids, and remember to burp them daily if you don't have fermentation lids with airlocks.

7. Once fermentation has occurred (between 3 and 7 days when you see bubbles at the top of the jar), you can place the jars in the fridge.

8. Once refrigerated, you can eat this immediately, but we tend to leave ours for 2 months in the fridge before eating because we like the flavor. But keep trying and tasting to see what works best for you.

Useful Tips

- When you reach the bottom of the jar of your sauerkraut, you could save the brine in the fridge to use in your next batch. It will help your next batch to ferment because of the bacteria in the brine.

- Put your jars on a plate or a tray so that if bubbles cause the brine to spill out of the jar, it won't create a mess.

4. Beet and Kohlrabi Sauerkraut

The color of this sauerkraut is beautiful—an orangey red, with bits of white and green in it—very vibrant and delicious looking. It tastes wonderful and is good for you because of the probiotics. You can use this sauerkraut as a condiment as well as in wraps or salads. This would be lovely on a bratwurst sausage.

Ingredients

- ½ head green cabbage, chopped
- 4 small beets, peeled and chopped
- 3 small kohlrabies, peeled and chopped
- 4 large carrots, grated
- 5 baby leeks, chopped
- 3 cloves garlic
- 1 inch (2.5 cm) ginger
- ¼ cup (60 ml) whey or ½ teaspoon vegetable culture starter
- Filtered water
- 2 teaspoons pickling, pure, kosher, or sea salt

Instructions

1. Peel and chop the vegetables into small chunks. Grate the carrots and ginger.
2. Place the vegetables in a bowl, and add the salt.
3. Ensure the vegetables are well mixed to help the salt draw out the water from them.
4. Fill the jars with the vegetable mixture.
5. Add the whey or vegetable culture starter to each jar.
6. Fill each jar with filtered water, ensuring the vegetables are submerged.
7. Weigh the vegetables down with a fermentation weight to stop the vegetables from floating. Leave 1 inch (2.5 cm) of headspace at the top of the jars. Fasten the lids on tightly.
8. Leave at room temperature for 7 days, then place in the fridge. Remember to burp the jars daily while they are fermenting if you don't have fermentation lids with airlocks.

5. Heirloom Sauerkraut

What makes this sauerkraut slightly different from the usual recipes is that it has a sweet and spicy taste, compared to traditional sauerkraut. This is a recipe that has been passed down through generations, which will give a healthy immune boost to anyone eating it. You can get the whole family involved in making sauerkraut, chopping the vegetables and fruits, pressing it down with a potato masher to get the vegetables to release their juices, and when it's ready, it can be eaten together as a family too (and shared with friends).

Ingredients

- 5 lb (2.3 kg) cabbage
- 1 onion

- 1 apple
- 1 red bell pepper
- ½ jalapeno pepper
- 2 cloves garlic
- 1 tablespoon fresh ginger root
- 3 tablespoons pickling, pure, kosher, or sea salt

Instructions

1. Finely chop the cabbage. Mince the garlic, and chop up the onion, apple, red bell pepper, jalapeno, and fresh ginger. Mix all of these together in a bowl.

2. Layer the cabbage and the fruit and veggie mix in a bowl—press it firmly with a potato masher after each layer.

3. Next, sprinkle the salt over the top, and mix this into the vegetables until the cabbage starts to release its juices.

4. Place this cabbage mixture in jars. Give the cabbage mixture a final press with the potato masher. You want enough liquid to cover the vegetables.

5. Weigh the sauerkraut down with fermentation weights, and let it ferment. You can cover the jar with a towel and let it ferment for 7–10 days. You can taste it after this time to see if you like the taste or want it to ferment further.

6. When it tastes like you want it to, place the jars in the fridge. Sauerkraut flavor does tend to improve with age in the fridge.

6. Kimchi

Kimchi is salted, seasoned, and fermented cabbage. It's a popular side dish in Korean cuisine. It has a lovely tangy and spicy taste. Kimchi can taste and smell quite strongly of garlic, so if you have a different fridge to store your kimchi in, it can stop the smell from seeping into other foods. Kimchi is traditionally made with Napa cabbage, and it has a lot of health benefits because the cabbage is so rich in vitamin C, which can help boost your immune system, help prevent heart disease, and is good for eye health too. The recipe below should take around 10 minutes to prepare and 20 minutes to make.

Ingredients

- 1 medium Napa cabbage
- 2 red jalapeno peppers
- ½ large radish
- ¼ large white onion
- 2 radishes for garnish
- 1 cup (240 ml) water
- 2 tablespoons pickling, pure, kosher, or sea salt
- ½ teaspoon sugar
- 6 cloves garlic
- 2 teaspoon red dried chili powder
- 1 teaspoon ginger
- ½ cup (24 g) chives
- 1 tablespoon cooked sweet rice

Instructions

1. Chop the cabbage into pieces.
2. Soak the cabbage for 2 hours in the water and salt.
3. Rinse the cabbage after soaking it in salt water using cold water.
4. Mix the radish, ginger, peppers, onion, red chili powder, garlic, cooked sweet rice, and sugar.
5. Add the mix to the cabbage.
6. Mix in the chopped chives.
7. Put this in airtight containers at room temperature for 24 hours.
8. After this time, move the jars to the fridge.

7. Green Cabbage Kimchi

This kimchi is delicious, spicy, crunchy, and salty. It can make a wonderful side dish if you don't happen to have salad ingredients in.

Ingredients

- 1 head green cabbage
- 3 bunches bok choy
- 3 green onions, sliced
- 1 cup (120 g) carrots, grated
- 1 cup (120 g) daikon radishes, grated
- 1½ tablespoons pickling, pure, kosher, or sea salt
- 10 cloves garlic
- 1-inch (2.5 cm) piece ginger
- 2 tablespoons red pepper flakes
- 1 tablespoon sesame seeds (optional)

Instructions

1. Chop the cabbage, bok choy, and green onions and place in a bowl. Grate the daikon and carrot into the bowl.
2. Mix the salt into the bowl, ensuring it's really worked through so that the cabbage starts to release its juices.
3. Mince the garlic, ginger, and pepper flakes, and stir these into the bowl.
4. Transfer this mixture to jars.
5. Ensure the vegetables are covered by the juices. Use fermentation weights to keep the vegetables submerged.
6. You can top off the jars with filtered water if you need to so long as all the ingredients are submerged. Cover the jars with lids, and remember to burp them every day if you don't have fermentation lids with airlocks.
7. Keep the jars at room temperature for 3–7 days, then refrigerate them.

8. Spicy Carrot Kimchi

This is a lovely vibrant kimchi that is bright and really stands out and makes food look appetizing. It has a spicy kick, and it's filled with probiotics that are great for your health. This kimchi is lovely served with Korean or other Asian-style dishes. You can mix some of this kimchi into rice (it goes well with sticky rice) or cooked grains. Kimchi gets stronger the longer it ferments, so it's usually best to eat this within 2 months.

Ingredients

- ¾ lb (340 g) carrots, peeled
- ¼ lb (113 g) daikon radishes, peeled
- 1 large scallion, white parts and half of the green parts, thinly sliced
- 3 cups (720 ml) filtered water
- 1½ tablespoons pickling, pure, kosher, or sea salt
- 1 teaspoon grated fresh ginger

- ½ teaspoon fish sauce or soy sauce
- ½ teaspoon red pepper flakes

Instructions

1. Place the salt and fish or soy sauce to filtered water.

2. Finely julienne (cut into long, thin strips) the carrots and daikon radishes into pieces approximately the size of a matchstick. If you have a mandoline or a thin slicing blade on a food processor, it will help.

3. Put the carrots, daikon radishes, ginger, scallion, and red pepper flakes in jars.

4. Pour over the brine. Ensure the carrots and radishes are fully submerged. If you need to use a glass weight to achieve this, do so.

5. Cover the jar loosely with a lid, but don't seal it completely. Put the jar onto a dish in case it overflows as it ferments.

6. Leave it at room temperature for 24–48 hours. After 24 hours, you should see some bubbles.

7. When the bubbles appear, then you can transfer the jar to the fridge where it will still ferment but slowly.

8. After 1–2 weeks, it will be ready to eat.

9. Chinese Pickled Cabbage

This is a quick pickle recipe that has crunchy Chinese cabbage, which is sweet and sour, similar to what is served at Chinese restaurants. In China, it is often served alongside millet, rice porridge, and steamed buns. It can also be served in restaurants before the main dish or as a palate cleanser.

Ingredients

- 1 lb (450 g) cabbage
- 1 large carrot
- 4 red chili peppers
- 1½ cups (360 ml) rice vinegar
- ½ cup (120 ml) water

- 2 tablespoons and 1 teaspoon pickling, pure, kosher, or sea salt
- ¾ cup (150 g) sugar
- 1 teaspoon Sichuan peppercorns
- 3 cloves garlic, crushed

Instructions

1. Place the water, rice vinegar, 1 teaspoon of salt, sugar, and chili peppers in a saucepan. Heat for around 5 minutes on a simmer to dissolve the sugar. Taste the pickling liquid to see if it's spicy enough for you. If you want it spicier, you can simmer it for longer.

2. Get rid of the core of the cabbage, and tear the leaves into bite-sized pieces. Cut the carrot into ¼-inch (6 mm) thick half-moon pieces.

3. Place the cabbage and carrots and 2 tablespoons of salt in a bowl, and toss all the vegetables with your hands to ensure they're all coated in salt. Leave them at room temperature for around 30 mins and up to an hour (but no more than an hour).

4. Drain the cabbage and carrots, and discard the salty water. Rinse the vegetables twice, drain them, and squeeze out the excess water. Put them in jars.

5. Add the crushed garlic and Sichuan peppercorns to the jars.

6. Pour the cooled pickling liquid into the jars. Try to keep the vegetables submerged—you can use a glass weight if needed.

7. Seal the jar, and keep it in the fridge pickling for 3 days. The sourness of the pickles will develop on the 3rd day.

8. Whenever you take any of the pickles out of the jar, use clean utensils (not hands).

9. You can keep these in the fridge for 2–3 weeks.

10. Red Pepper and Cabbage Pickle

This recipe is lovely as a side salad with sandwiches or cold meat. If you want a spicier flavor, you could also add in a jalapeno pepper to each jar.

Ingredients

- 2 heads cabbage, finely shredded
- 10 onions, chopped
- 10 sweet red peppers, chopped
- 4 cups (960 ml) vinegar
- 4 cups (960 ml) water
- 1 cup (240 ml) vegetable oil
- 3 tablespoons pickling, pure, kosher, or sea salt
- 1½ cups (300 g) white sugar
- 1 tablespoon mustard seeds
- 1 tablespoon ground turmeric
- 1 tablespoon celery seed

Instructions

1. Put the finely shredded cabbage in a bowl, and sprinkle the salt over it, then toss it with your hands to ensure all the cabbage is covered with salt.

2. Put plastic wrap over the top of the bowl, and place it in a refrigerator overnight for at least 8 hours to let it soak in.

3. Drain the cabbage, and squeeze the liquid out so that it's as dry as possible.

4. Put the water, vinegar, sugar, vegetable oil, mustard seeds, and turmeric in a saucepan, and bring it to a boil.

5. Stir in the drained cabbage, onions, and red pepper, and bring up to a boil again. Reduce to a simmer for 45 minutes until the onions are tender.

6. Sterilize 6 quart (0.95 L) jars and lids by boiling them in water for 5 minutes. Then place the cabbage mixture into the hot jars, leaving about 1 inch (2.5 cm) of headspace. Cover the jars with lids, and screw on the rings.

7. Place the jars into a large pot. Fill it halfway with water. Ensure the jars are covered by 1 inch (2.5 cm) of water, bring to a boil, then cover the pot and process for 25 minutes.

8. Remove the jars from the pot and place onto a cloth surface until they cool. Press the top of each lid with a finger, ensuring that the seal is tight (the lids should not move up or down at all). Store in a cool, dark area.

Key takeaways from this chapter:

1. Traditional sauerkraut only has two ingredients, cabbage and salt.

2. It's a good idea to store kimchi in a different fridge because it may seep in with its strong garlic smell and permeate other food in the fridge.

3. A mandoline is a good tool to slice beets, apples, and cabbage for sauerkraut.

4. If you get stained by beets, salt and lemon juice are good to remove this.

5. Sauerkraut is best eaten cold because if you heat it, this would kill the probiotics.

6. You can include whey in sauerkraut recipes, because it's rich in lactic acid.

7. If you save the brine from your sauerkraut, you can use it to help ferment the next batch, due to the bacteria in it.

8. Place fermentation jars onto a plate or tray so that bubbles from the brine do not spill over and cause a mess.

The next chapter will focus on relishes, chutneys, salsas, and other condiments. Fantastic recipes that make great accompaniments to meals, transforming them completely and really levelling them up with the addition of a good chutney, salsa, or sauce. There are a few spreads and dips mentioned too, and the most amazing fermented hot sauce, which is easy to make and truly delicious!

Chapter 7: Relishes, Chutneys, Salsas, Sauces, and Other Condiments

This chapter covers salsas, condiments, sauces, relishes, chutneys, and hot sauces. The perfect condiments to level up your meals and make them taste delicious. Condiments make a lovely accompaniment and really bring out the flavors of food by adding sweetness, acidity, or some heat. All of these condiments make fantastic gifts to give to friends and family to liven up their meal times too.

Relishes, Chutneys, Salsas, Sauces, and Other Condiments Recipes

1. Fiery Fermented Tomato Salsa

When you're having a movie night with friends or family, is there anything better than some tortilla chips dipped in lovely salsa? This salsa is fiery, with some real heat to warm you up on a winter evening. It's a great way to preserve food. If you're growing your own tomatoes and onions and you have an abundance of them, making this delicious salsa is perfect. You can use the salsa as a nice appetizer on a summer afternoon picnic or a BBQ too. This can be whipped up and eaten fairly swiftly so long as the salsa has fermented for at least 48 hours.

Ingredients

- 2 lb (900 g) tomatoes, chopped
- 1 onion, finely diced
- 2 jalapeno peppers, finely diced
- 1 teaspoon pickling, pure, kosher, or sea salt
- 2 garlic cloves, minced
- 1 tablespoon lime juice
- ¼ cup (4 g) cilantro (coriander), chopped

Instructions

1. Mix all the ingredients in a bowl and stir thoroughly.

2. Put them into a quart (0.95L) jar, leaving ½ inch (1.2 cm) of space at the top of the jar.

3. Put a lid on the jar and store somewhere clean and cool, perhaps in a pantry or a kitchen cupboard.

4. After 24 hours, you may see bubbles appearing. If any white film appears on the top—this is kahm yeast, which is safe, and it's normal for this to occur.

5. After 48 hours, it should be fermented. You can stir the jar so that the solids mix back in with the liquid.

6. Refrigerate the jar, and use it up within 2 weeks.

2. Fermented Pico de Gallo Salsa

This is a very simple recipe with few ingredients, and it's ready after just 48 hours! This recipe will give you a mild salsa, unlike the previous one, which is hot. Salsa is great to dip tortilla chips or nachos into. You can also have salsa as an accompaniment to meat, fish, scrambled eggs, and vegetables. It's good to try and include some fermented food with each meal, so salsa makes a nice addition.

Ingredients

- 4 large tomatoes
- 1 onion
- 2 teaspoons pickling, pure, kosher, or sea salt
- 2 tablespoons lime juice
- 2 cups (32 g) cilantro (coriander) leaves

Instructions

1. Chop the tomatoes, onion, and cilantro (coriander).
2. Add the salt and lime juice.
3. Put the salsa mix in a jar, and ensure that the liquid covers all of the vegetables. Cover the jar with a lid.
4. Place the jar in a cupboard that is cool and dark for 48 hours. When you stir it, you may see bubbles, which shows it has fermented.
5. Keep it in the fridge after this time and use within 4–5 days.

3. Fermented Salsa

This salsa not only tastes delicious and looks amazing, but it is also gluten free and vegan. So, if you or your friends or family are gluten free or vegan, this can make a wonderful gift to give them and can really jazz up meals by adding a delicious tangy condiment.

I'm a huge fan of salsa—it accompanies meat, fish, vegetable dishes, and tortilla chips so well. It's a great way to use up harvested vegetables and preserve them.

If you use whey, it will reduce the amount of time it takes to ferment. If you don't want to use whey, then you can double the amount of salt. You can adjust the vegetables in the salsa depending on what vegetables you have growing in your garden or what is available at your local farmer's market. You could eat this with crisps, chips, crackers, on salads, with eggs, steamed veggies, soups, and more.

Ingredients

- 3 lb (1.35 kg) organic tomatoes
- 1 onion
- 2–3 peppers (Your choice as to quantity and type of peppers. I like spicy, so I usually go with 2 serrano and 1 jalapeno. You can use bell peppers if you like your salsa mild.)
- 4 cloves garlic
- 1 bunch fresh cilantro (coriander)
- Juice from 2 limes or lemons
- 2 tablespoons whey
- 1 tablespoon pickling, pure, kosher, or sea salt (double the amount if you don't use whey)
- Dried spices (such as chipotle, chili powder, and cumin)

Instructions

1. You can either chop or gently pulse tomatoes in a food processor (but most people want a bit of chunkiness to the salsa).
2. Put the chopped tomatoes, chopped onion, peppers, herbs, and spices in a bowl.

3. Add in the lime or lemon juice and the salt and mix well.

4. Place this mixture in glass jars, remembering to leave an inch (2.5 cm) of headspace.

5. Put the lids on the jars.

6. Leave on the counter for 3 days at room temperature before transferring to the fridge.

7. You can keep the salsa in the fridge for a few months, and the flavors will intensify over time.

4. Honey Fermented Ginger

Both honey and ginger have incredible healing properties. Honey has natural antiseptic properties and is very soothing, and ginger is warming. Both have anti-inflammatory properties, and the probiotics will give your gut health a boost too. Both are excellent to combat colds and flu. When you ferment honey and ginger together, you get a lovely syrup that you can drizzle into your tea or on top of porridge, pancakes, crumpets, and more. This shouldn't take you longer than 5 minutes to make, and it's really delicious. Quite literally, all you have to do is put honey and ginger in the jar and then let them do their thing while you just wait. Raw honey contains natural yeast and bacteria, so when you add water to this, it will start to ferment (this is similar to how mead is made but with more water—this will be covered in Chapter 10). There will likely be no bubbles (although you may get small bubbles on the surface of the honey), and you don't need to burp the jars for this recipe because the ferment takes place slowly.

Ingredients

- 1 cup (340 g) raw honey (Pasteurized honey will not ferment. Honey bought from a shop may be pasteurized to give it a better shelf life, but this destroys the bacteria and yeast within it, so it will not ferment.)

- Organic ginger, peeled and roughly chopped (Again, important to know it's organic because non-organic may be irradiated to destroy the yeast. It should be fresh and moist. A tip to help peel the ginger is to take a spoon and use the side of it to scrape the skin off the ginger—it will give you much more ginger, without you lopping big bits off it with a knife. You can easily maneuver the spoon around the knobbly bits too.)

Instructions

1. Chop your peeled ginger into pieces—this will help the honey to have a lot of surface area that it can get to so that the sugar from the honey can start the fermentation process.

2. Put the ginger into a sterilized jar—ensure you fill it halfway full of ginger.

3. Then pour the honey into the jar, ensuring it covers all the ginger, plus an inch (2.5 cm) higher.

4. Leave a couple of inches (5 cm) at the top of the jar because once the ginger starts to break down a little, it will release water, and this will increase the liquid level in the jar. The ginger will float to the top eventually—this is normal.

5. Stir the jar with a clean wooden spoon every day for 2 weeks.

6. The ginger will become a darker color, and the honey will become thinner. There may be small bubbles appearing on the surface of the honey.

7. After 2 weeks, dip a teaspoon in and try it. If you like it, seal it, and place it in the fridge. If you want

it stronger, leave it for a further 2 weeks before refrigerating. (We personally don't tend to refrigerate our honey/ginger mix because it is slow to ferment and it gets used up quickly, then we make a new batch.

8. You can use the honey/ginger mix as part of a salad dressing, for marinades, and it's lovely over roast chicken or other meats. You could also have some of this syrup in smoothies or cocktails or in a hot toddy if you have a cold/flu. It's a lovely drizzle over yogurts or ice cream, or mixed into apple crumbles, and as mentioned earlier, I have it in cups of tea.

9. You can use this same recipe but put different fruit in there instead of the ginger—you could have peaches, cherries, pears, raspberries, blackberries, apples, elderberries, and so on. Another unusual but tasty variation is honey fermented garlic.

5. Pickled Nasturtium Seeds (Poor Man's Capers)

Pickled nasturtium seeds give a pop of flavor to dishes. They are sometimes called poor man's capers, but they do make a really good substitute. They are wonderful stirred into salad dressings or sprinkled on pasta. They are also a nice addition to cheese boards. Nasturtium seeds have a strong peppery flavor that can be potent, but when fermented, they develop a nice vinegary flavor, just like capers.

When you harvest nasturtium seeds, you do need to ensure that the plants haven't been sprayed with chemical pesticides (it's okay if they've been sprayed with organic pesticides, like neem oil or insecticidal soap), and also don't take all the seeds so that the plants can reseed themselves. Clean the seeds, and

break them up (as they'll often clump together). Essentially, all you have to do is place them in a jar and pour some salt brine over them. You will then need to drain the brine and cover them with a fresh brine. But I'll explain this in more detail below.

Ingredients

- 1 cup (8 oz or 240 ml) freshly harvested nasturtium seed pods
- 4 teaspoons pickling, pure, kosher, or sea salt
- 2 cups (480 ml) filtered water

Instructions

1. Pick your seeds.
2. Wash them thoroughly, and break clumped seed pods apart, also remove the stems.
3. Place the seeds in a jar.
4. Dissolve the salt in the water to make a brine and pour over the nasturtium seeds to cover them.
5. Use a fermentation glass weight to keep the seeds submerged in the brine and stop them from floating to the surface.
6. Put a lid on the jar, and allow it to sit at room temperature for 3 days. If you don't have a fermentation lid with an airlock, remember to burp the jar daily.
7. After 3 days, the jar may smell of sulfur—this is normal. Drain the seeds, and cover them with fresh brine, and allow the jar to sit at room temperature for 3 more days.
8. After this time, you can taste a seed to see if you like how fermented it is.

Once it has fermented to a taste that you like, place the jar in the fridge.

6. Fermented Cranberry Sauce

This is the perfect condiment to accompany holiday get-togethers of Thanksgiving and Christmas—it's perfect with turkey! This sauce has maple, figs, citrus, and cloves, which makes it have a delicious festive spice, and it's perfect on meat, salmon, and with salads. It doesn't contain any refined sugar, which can be good for people following a paleo diet. It's good and fermented, which will give you lots of healthy probiotics. Cranberries themselves contain high vitamin C, and they're anti-inflammatory and full of antioxidants. Once fermented, the cranberries will be less sharp.

This recipe does need to be anaerobic (without air), so the fruit needs to be weighed down to stay below the brine to allow it to become fermented and prevent mold. Glass fermenting weights are an ideal solution for this. Having an airlock lid will also prevent any oxygen getting inside the jar. Or if you don't wish to do it that way, you could purchase a crock. It should take around 20 minutes in total to prepare.

Ingredients

- 5 cups (580 g) fresh cranberries
- ½ cup (75 g) dried figs
- ½ cup (75 g) raisins
- ¼ cup (60 ml) brine from a prior ferment or whey
- Juice of 1 orange and 2 teaspoons of its zest
- Juice of 1 lemon and 1 teaspoon of its zest
- ½ cup (170 g) maple syrup
- 1 cup (240 ml) filtered water
- 1 teaspoon pickling, pure, kosher, or sea salt
- 1 cinnamon stick
- ⅛ teaspoon ground cloves

Instructions

1. Put the cranberries into a food processor until they're minced. Place them into a fermentation crock or a bowl and put to one side for now.

2. Put the rest of the ingredients, excluding the brine and cinnamon stick, into the food processor. Pulse them until they are chopped small but not a puree.

3. Add these to the crock or large bowl with the cranberries, then stir in the brine.

4. Spoon this into sterilized jars if you're not using a crock, and weigh the contents down so that the brine is covering it all. Put the lid on.

5. Leave them in a warm place for 3–5 days. You will start to see bubbles appear, and it will look bubbly once fermentation is complete.

6. Place in the fridge and store for up to a month.

7. Fermented Hot Sauce

When hot sauce is made with fermented peppers, it will have a lot more depth of flavor than sauces that are made with fresh peppers. If you ferment your peppers for 4 months before turning them into a sauce, it will give you a phenomenal taste. It's a great way to use up chili peppers at the end of a growing season. Many well-known hot sauces, like Tabasco and Sriracha, are made with fermented peppers. Hot sauce can be added to eggs, rice dishes, meat, casseroles, chicken wings, nachos, pasta, tacos, and more. You can put some drops into mayonnaise, aioli, or ketchup to spice them up with fries, pizza, or on a sandwich.

Any types of peppers can be used to make a hot sauce. If you want it to be a mild hot sauce, then you could use poblano or Fresno peppers and perhaps add some bell peppers to ensure it's not too hot. If you want your hot sauce to be of medium intensity, then using jalapeno, serrano, Hungarian wax, red cherry, or cayenne peppers would be preferable. If you want an extra hot sauce, then you can use scotch bonnet, dragon's breath, or ghost peppers, but these will create an extremely hot sauce. Using a mix of peppers will give the sauce a more complex flavor.

You will need quart (0.95L) canning jars, fermentation lids, fermentation weights to ensure the food is submerged under the brine, and ideally a pH meter to see if the peppers have reached the right acidity to make the sauce (it should ideally be around 3.5).

Ingredients

- Fermented pepper mash (from a regular fermented pepper recipe and can be done over weeks, months, or years—the flavor changes over time, becoming more acidic and pungent). You can find fermented jalapenos recipe in Chapter 4 (recipe number 9), and you can also ferment other hot peppers using this recipe. If you have only fermented your peppers for a few weeks, you may need to add vinegar to the hot sauce to ensure the pH is below 3.7 (ideally 3.5), which makes it safe to store.

- Crushed garlic

- You can optionally add in carrots, onion, celery, and other vegetables to give your sauce your own special take.

Instructions

1. Put the fermented pepper mash into a large saucepan with the crushed garlic, and bring it to a boil, then reduce to simmer. If you want a sweeter sauce similar to Sriracha, then add brown sugar or honey.

2. Cook this for 30 minutes to an hour over a low heat.

3. Put the cooked peppers into a blender, and process them. If you want a smooth sauce, you can puree it until smooth.

4. Place the sauce into sterilized bottles using a funnel.

5. Put the cap on the bottles. The sauce will become stronger with age.

6. You can refrigerate the bottle, or if you have a pressure canner, you could use that to make them

shelf stable, but it would change the flavor slightly and kill off the probiotics. The sauce should keep for up to a year in the fridge.

8. Fermented Mango Habanero Hot Sauce

Sauces that contain fruit are really delicious and zingy. They manage to be sweet and spicy, and because they've been fermented, you know that they have a healthy amount of probiotics in the sauce too. I adore this sauce, and it's hard not to put it on everything! I adore its vibrant yellow color too, guaranteed to liven up any salad! It's important to wear gloves when handling peppers to avoid them burning your skin. Also, avoid rubbing your face after handling them—wash your hands thoroughly first.

Ingredients

- 2 large mangoes, peeled and chopped
- 1 large habanero pepper
- ¼ cup (60 ml) apple cider vinegar
- ¼ cup (85 g) honey
- 1 teaspoon pickling, pure, kosher, or sea salt
- 2 tablespoons whey (if you can't or don't want to use whey, you can substitute this for a vegetable-based starter culture)
- 3 cloves garlic
- ½ teaspoon cumin
- ¼ teaspoon white pepper

Instructions

1. Remove the seeds from the pepper.
2. Coarsely chop the pepper.
3. Combine all ingredients, then blend everything together until smooth.
4. Place in a glass jar and cover with a cheesecloth or a cotton towel. Secure this with a rubber band.
5. Allow it to ferment at room temperature for 12 hours.
6. Next, refrigerate until it is ready to use.
7. You can keep this in the fridge for up to 6 months.

9. Banana Pepper Hot Sauce

This is a lovely spicy condiment that is full of flavor and probiotics and is really easy to make. As the banana peppers age and the flavors combine with the tang of the brine, it creates a harmonious sauce. Once you've created the sauce, it's good to keep it in a flip-top bottle in the fridge so that you can use it on your favorite dishes. Banana peppers are great and easy to grow, so if you plant some, you can keep on making a lovely supply of banana pepper hot sauce for yourself, your family, and your friends. This sauce would be perfect to use on tacos, stirred into chili, or used as seasoning when cooking things that need a little additional flavor.

Ingredients

- 4 cups (520 g) banana peppers, with stems removed
- 2½ tablespoons pickling, pure, kosher, or sea salt
- 2 cloves garlic
- Filtered/distilled water

Instructions

1. Pack the peppers and garlic into a jar.
2. Add the salt into the jar.
3. Pour over water so that it covers everything in the jar.
4. Use a fermentation weight to keep the peppers submerged below the brine.
5. Seal the jar, and let it ferment at room temperature for 4 weeks.
6. During the first 2 weeks, burp the jar daily if you don't have a fermentation lid with an airlock.
7. After 4 weeks, the peppers should taste tangy and be fermented.
8. You can place them in the fridge for a few months until you're ready to use them.
9. When you want to turn the peppers into hot sauce, place the peppers, garlic, and ⅓ of the brine into a blender and blend. If the sauce is too thick, then add some more brine. When you taste it, if you feel it needs some more salt or apple cider vinegar, you could add these to give it a little more kick.
10. You can then keep the hot sauce bottled in the fridge for weeks.

10. Fermented Ketchup

Ketchup is delicious on fries, meat, burgers, or on a cheese toasty—many people put it on almost everything, and I have to agree, it does make most food extra tasty. This fermented ketchup is really easy to make, and it's a healthier alternative to store-bought without all the unneeded (and unhealthy) ingredients.

Ingredients

- 12 oz (340 g) organic tomato paste
- ⅓ cup (80 ml) filtered water
- 2 tablespoons whey
- 2 tablespoons raw apple cider vinegar
- 2 tablespoons raw organic honey
- ½ teaspoon pickling, pure, kosher, or sea salt
- ¼ teaspoon mustard
- ⅛ teaspoon allspice

Instructions

1. Mix all the ingredients in a bowl.
2. Transfer this to a glass jar.
3. Fasten the jar with a lid.
4. Leave on a kitchen counter for 3 days. Remember to burp the jar daily if you don't have a fermentation lid with an airlock.
5. Then transfer the jar to the fridge.

11. Apple Raisin Chutney

This is a delicious chutney that goes well with chicken, pork chops, ham, or with a cheese board. It's also nice on a cheese sandwich.

Ingredients

- 4 pink lady or honey crisp apples (approximately 1.5 lb or 680 g)
- 1 medium yellow onion, finely chopped
- 1 cup (150 g) raisins
- ⅓ cup (80 ml) apple cider vinegar
- ¼ cup (60 ml) red wine vinegar
- 2½ tablespoons lemon juice
- ⅔ cup (133 g) white sugar
- ¼ cup (50 g) light brown sugar
- ¾ teaspoon pickling, pure, kosher, or sea salt
- ⅓ cup (32 g) fresh ginger
- 3 cloves garlic, minced
- 3 cinnamon sticks
- 1 teaspoon paprika powder
- ¾ teaspoon fresh grated nutmeg
- ½ teaspoon ground cloves
- ½ teaspoon ground black pepper
- ¼ teaspoon allspice

Instructions

1. This recipe is really simple. Place all the ingredients into a large saucepan. Bring it to a boil, then reduce the heat to a low simmer.

2. Keep cooking this mixture, stirring it from time to time, until the chutney has reduced and is thick. This will take about 2 hours, which may seem a long time, but it's definitely worth it.

3. The chutney can be served hot or cold.

12. Mango Chutney

This chutney is tangy, sweet, and savory, and it's easy to make. It can be canned for longer storage. This chutney goes really well with pork dishes, such as pork chops. It's also the perfect accompaniment to other cold meats, like chicken or lamb. You can also use it as a glaze for chicken or duck. It's nice with cheese or on sandwiches too. This chutney is spicy and sweet. Ginger, mustard seeds, garlic, and red chili pepper flakes give it spice. The tang comes from the acidity in mangoes and vinegar. And the sweetness comes from mangoes, raisins, and sugar.

Ingredients

- 5 large ripe mangoes (approximately 3.5 lb or 1.6 kg), peeled and cut into ¾-inch (2 cm) pieces.
- 1 medium onion, chopped
- ½ cup (75 g) golden raisins
- ¼ cup (45 g) crystallized ginger, finely chopped
- 1 cup (240 ml) white vinegar
- 2 cups (400 g) sugar
- 1 clove garlic, minced
- 1 teaspoon whole mustard seeds
- ¼ teaspoon red pepper flakes

Instructions

1. Place the sugar and vinegar in a saucepan, bring to a boil, and stir until the sugar has dissolved.

2. Add all the other ingredients, and turn the heat down to a simmer, have the saucepan uncovered, and cook for approximately 45 minutes to 1 hour, stirring from time to time, until the mixture is syrupy in appearance and has thickened.

3. Pour it into sterilized jars, leaving ½ inch (1.2 cm) of space at the top. Close the jars with lids.

4. If you wish to water-bath them to make them more shelf stable, then put a rack on the bottom of a large pot. Put the sealed jars on the rack. Fill the pot with water, ensuring the jars are covered

with 1 inch (2.5 cm) of water. Bring to a rolling boil and boil for 15 minutes.

5. Carefully remove the jars, and let them cool at room temperature.

6. If you don't want to water-bath the mango chutney, you don't have to—you can keep it refrigerated in a jar covered with a lid for up to a month. You may also freeze jars of mango chutney—leave an inch (2.5 cm) at the top of the jar to allow the frozen contents to expand. They will keep in the freezer for up to 3 months.

13. Cucumber Relish

This relish is easy to make and is amazing on hot dogs. For this recipe, you will need 2 quart (0.95L) or 4 pint (473 ml) canning jars with lids and rings.

Ingredients

- 7 large cucumbers
- 4 large sweet onions
- 3 cups (720 ml) distilled white vinegar
- ¼ cup (70 g) pickling, pure, kosher, or sea salt
- 3 cups (600 g) white sugar
- 1 cup (240 ml) filtered water
- ½ cup (60 g) all-purpose flour (you can use ⅓ cup (40 g) cornstarch instead of flour)
- 1 teaspoon celery seed
- 1 teaspoon ground turmeric
- 1 teaspoon ground ginger (if you're not keen on ginger, you can leave it out)
- You can add ground mustard and mustard seeds if you like mustard

Instructions

1. Grate the cucumbers and onions on a large grater setting into a bowl.

2. Sprinkle the salt over the vegetables. Cover the bowl with plastic wrap and leave at room temperature for 8 hours overnight.

3. Drain the cucumber and onion mixture, and squeeze out as much liquid from it as possible. Place this to one side.

4. In a different bowl, add the sugar, flour, turmeric, ginger, and celery seed.

5. In a large saucepan, heat the vinegar and water.

6. Stir the sugar and flour mixture into the vinegar and water until smooth.

7. Next, stir in the cucumber and onion.

8. Bring this to a boil and cook, stirring it frequently, until the relish has thickened. This will take approximately 15 minutes.

9. Sterilize your jars and lids by boiling them in water for at least 5 minutes.

10. Place the relish in the hot sterilized jars, leaving at least ¼ inch (6 mm) of space at the top. Put the lids on, and screw on the rings.

11. Place a rack in the bottom of a large stockpot and fill halfway with water. Bring to a boil. Lower in the jars using a holder. Leave 2 inches (5 cm) of space between the jars, and make sure the jars are

covered by at least an inch (2.5 cm) of water. Bring the water to a full boil, cover the pot, and process the jars for 10 minutes.

12. Take out the jars and place on a cloth covered or wooden surface, ensuring the jars have some space between them. Let them cool.

13. Press the top of each lid to ensure the seal is tight.

14. Store in a cool, dark area.

14. Onion Relish

This is a great, vibrant, pink-looking relish that is delicious on BBQ food in the spring and summer. It's perfect for hot dogs, burgers, and steaks. This makes a wonderful condiment, and it's nice to give to others as a gift.

Ingredients

- ½ cup (60 g) red onion, cut into thin slivers
- ½ cup (60 g) white onion, cut into thin slivers
- ¼ cup (45 g) green bell pepper, julienned (cut into long, thin strips)
- ½ cup (120 ml) white vinegar
- 1 tablespoon white sugar

Instructions

1. Put the vinegar and sugar in a saucepan and heat gently until the sugar has dissolved.

2. Turn off the heat. Add the red onion, white onion, and bell pepper and stir. Then let it sit for 1 hour.

3. After 1 hour, transfer the mixture to jars and refrigerate for at least 2 hours before consuming.

15. Sweet Balsamic Onion Relish

This relish is quick and easy to make. And it's delicious on burgers as well as with eggs and grilled mushrooms, and it makes a fantastic topping for sandwiches or pizzas.

Ingredients

- 4 yellow onions, cut into slices or diced, whichever is your preference
- ½ cup (120 ml) balsamic vinegar
- ⅓ cup (67 g) sugar
- 1 teaspoon coconut or olive oil

Instructions

1. Slice or chop the onions. Put them in a frying pan with the coconut or olive oil.

2. Cook the onions gently until they're soft for approximately 15–20 minutes.

3. Put the onions in a saucepan. Add the sugar and vinegar to the cooked onions and cook on low heat for about an hour until the onions have cooked down and the balsamic vinegar has reduced.

4. Strain the onions, and place them in a jar, discarding the vinegar.

5. You can keep the jar for up to a week in the refrigerator.

One of my favorite recipes from this chapter is the honey fermented ginger. But the honey fermented ginger is a wonderful thing to have in the house—absolutely perfect for the winter months because it's so soothing and has wonderful healing properties for cold and flu. It's also wonderful on top of toast, porridge, and pancakes. It makes a lovely gift to give people too.

Key takeaways from this chapter:

1. When you need to peel ginger, you can use a tablespoon to peel the skin off.

2. If you ferment peppers at least 4 months before making hot sauce, this will give your sauce a phenomenal taste.

3. Sriracha sauce is made from peppers that were fermented for years.

4. If you don't want to use whey in recipes, you can use a vegetable-based starter culture.

5. If you want to process jars to make them more shelf stable, you can use the water bath canning method—put them on a rack and cover with an inch (2.5 cm) of water, bring the water to a rolling boil, and boil them at least 10 minutes.

The next chapter will focus on pickled meat, fish, and eggs. I think it is an interesting chapter because not everyone thinks immediately of pickling meat, fish, or eggs. But these are wonderful to pickle, and it's another great way to preserve food to have all year round. The chapter covers pickled pork, beef, sausage, and eggs as well as pickled and fermented fish.

Chapter 8: Pickled Meat, Fish, and Eggs

This chapter looks at pickling meat, fish, and eggs. Quite unusual compared to the usual pickles, chutneys, salsas, kimchi, and sauerkraut—it's not what immediately springs to mind. But there are certainly some tasty recipes included here that are well worth trying.

Pickled Meat, Fish, and Eggs Recipes

1. Pickled Pork

There's a wonderful dish called New Orleans red beans and rice, and it's made with pickled meat. It can be hard to find pickled meat in shops, so it's great to be able to make your own.

Ingredients

- 2 lb (900 g) fresh pork (you can use pork chops or ham and cut the chunks into 2-inch-thick (5 cm) pieces)
- ½ medium onion, chopped
- 4 cups (800 g) white vinegar
- 1 tablespoon pickling, pure, kosher, or sea salt
- 1 tablespoon black peppercorns
- 6 cloves garlic
- 6 whole allspice berries
- 6 whole cloves
- 3 bay leaves
- ½ cup (53 g) mustard seeds
- 1 pinch pink meat cure
- ½ teaspoon crushed red pepper or cayenne pepper

Instructions

1. Place all the ingredients except the pork into a large saucepan, bring it to a boil, and boil for 4 minutes. Then place it in a container to cool in the fridge. Once it's cooled down completely, add the pork.
2. Ensure the pork is completely covered by the brine.
3. Cover and keep in the fridge for 4 days before you start to eat it.
4. If you have any pickled meat left, you could vacuum seal or tightly wrap it and freeze it for future use. You can then cook with this and add it to things like beans or cabbage. It's tender and tastes a bit like ham but even more delicious. It's ideal for adding to crock pots.

2. New England-Style Pickled Beef

Pickled beef is made by soaking it in a salt solution, and this is what helps keep the brisket moist. It makes a wonderful boiled dinner that your whole family will enjoy.

Ingredients

- 4.5 lb (2 kg) beef brisket, trimmed
- 9 small red potatoes, quartered
- 6 small onions, peeled and halved
- 2 lb (900 g) cabbage, cored and quartered
- 1½ cups (180 g) carrot, cut into 2-inch-thick (5 cm) slices
- 7 cups (1.68L) water
- ¾ cup (210 g) pickling, pure, kosher, or sea salt
- ½ cup (100 g) sugar
- 4 garlic cloves, crushed
- 8 bay leaves
- 6 sprigs thyme

- 2 tablespoons pickling spice

- 2 tablespoons black peppercorns

- 1 tablespoon juniper berries, crushed

- 1 tablespoon coriander seed

- 2 cups (480 ml or 440 g) ice cubes

Instructions

1. Put 1 cup (240 ml) of water, plus the peppercorns, pickling spice, juniper berries, coriander seeds, bay leaves, thyme sprigs, and garlic cloves into a small saucepan and bring to a boil. Reduce the heat and simmer for 5 minutes. Then pour into a bowl, letting it cool at room temperature.

2. Add 6 cups (1.44L) of water, salt, and sugar, and stir until the salt and sugar have dissolved. Pour this mixture into a 2-gallon (7.8L) plastic bag or tub, add the ice and brisket, and seal. Keep in the fridge for 3 days, turning it occasionally. After 3 days, remove the brisket, and discard the brine. Dry the brisket with paper towels.

3. Put the brisket in a stockpot. Cover it with water, and bring it to a boil, skimming the foam from the surface. Cover, reduce heat, and simmer for 2.5–3 hours until the brisket is tender. Remove it from the pan, keeping the cooking liquid in the pan. Add the carrots, cabbage, potatoes, and onions to the cooking liquid and bring to a boil, then turn down the heat and simmer them for 30 minutes or until they are tender.

3. Homemade Corned Beef

This recipe makes a delicious meat to accompany potatoes and vegetables. You may decide to let the corned beef cool and use it in sandwiches or as part of a salad. It goes nicely with mac and cheese and other pasta dishes. For St. Patrick's Day, it is notoriously served with cabbage.

Ingredients

- 5 lb (2.27 kg) beef brisket

- 2 carrots

- 1 onion

- 2 stalks celery

- 4 cloves garlic

- 1 ounce (30 g) pink curing salt (if you choose not to use a pink salt (that contains nitrate), you can use regular salt, but the corned beef would be grey in color rather than red)

- 1½ cups (420 g) pickling, pure, kosher, or sea salt

- ½ cup (100 g) brown sugar

- 1 packet pickling spice

- 16 cups (3.84L) filtered water

Instructions

1. Rinse the brisket, and pat it dry with paper towels.

2. If you want to trim off excess fat from the meat, you can.

3. In a saucepan, put 4 cups (960 ml) of water, and add the salt, sugar, pink salt, and pickling spice. Bring this to a boil.

4. Mince 3 cloves of garlic and add to the pot.

5. Once boiled, reduce the heat, and let it simmer, stirring until the sugar and salt have dissolved.

6. Put the brine into a container large enough to hold the brisket but one that can fit in the fridge. Add 12 cups (2.88L) of cold water to this.

7. Let the mixture cool before putting the brisket in it. You can use a plate or a tray to weigh down the brisket and keep it submerged under the brine. Then cover this with plastic wrap.

8. Let the brisket cure in the brine for a minimum of 5 days and a maximum of 10.

9. After the brisket has cured, lift it out of the brine, discard the brine, and rinse the brisket thoroughly with cool running water.

10. Put the brisket into a large saucepan or pot, and cover it with water. Add the remaining pickling spice and bring to a boil.

11. While it's coming to a boil, prepare the carrots and celery stalks, and add them to the pot.

12. Peel and quarter the onion, and mince the remaining clove of garlic, and add these to the pot.

13. After it has boiled, half cover the pot with a lid, and reduce heat so that it's simmering. Let it cook for 3–4 hours until it's tender and a fork can easily go into the brisket.

14. Once cooked, you can put the brisket on a cutting board. If you want to cover it in foil to keep it warm while you finish other parts of the meal, you can.

15. When you want to eat it, you can cut the beef against the grain. If you want some corned beef for sandwiches, let it come to room temperature after cooking, then place in the fridge to chill before slicing it. Enjoy!

4. Chinese Pickled Beef

Ingredients

- 1⅓ (600 g) beef shank
- 1.3 gallons (5 L) water
- 5 oz (150 ml) dark rice wine
- 3.3 oz (100 ml) soy sauce
- 8 tablespoons light soy sauce
- 3 tablespoons pickling, pure, kosher, or sea salt
- ¼ cup (50 g) cane sugar
- ½ cup (50 g) ginger
- 3 leeks
- 3 cardamom pods
- 3 cloves
- 2 dried chilies
- 2 star anise
- 2 bay leaves
- 1 nutmeg
- 1 teaspoon mixed pepper
- ½ teaspoon coriander seeds
- ½ teaspoon fennel seeds
- 2 tablespoons soybean paste
- Lemon zest

For Sauce

- 2 cloves garlic
- 2 teaspoons beef stock
- 2 teaspoons rice vinegar
- 1 teaspoon sesame oil
- 1 tablespoon light soy sauce
- 1 pinch salt
- 1 pinch pepper

To Serve

- 1 cucumber
- Cilantro (coriander)
- Chili

Instructions

1. Remove the bones, sinew, and skin from the beef. Season it with salt, and allow it to rest for 4 hours.

2. Put 2 quarts (1.9L) of the water in a saucepan, plus the cardamom, star anise, bay leaves, chilis, cloves, coriander, nutmeg, pepper, fennel seeds, lemon

zest, rice wine, soy sauce, soybean paste. and sugar and bring it to a boil.

3. Place the beef in a large pot with the remaining water, and bring it to a boil.

4. Finely chop the ginger and leeks.

5. Place the ginger, leeks, and beef into the stock. If you need to add more water, then do so. Bring it to a boil before turning down the heat and simmering on a medium heat for 1.5 hours.

6. Let it cool. Next, transfer it to the fridge for 12 hours.

7. You can slice the beef, then make a sauce to drizzle over it out of 2 cloves of garlic, 2 teaspoons of rice vinegar, 1 teaspoon of sesame oil, 1 tablespoon of light soy sauce, 2 tablespoons of beef stock, a pinch of salt, and a pinch of pepper. Simply mix these together.

8. Put cucumber, cilantro, and chili on the top before serving.

5. Pickled Beef Tongue or Brisket

In this recipe, well known at Jewish delis, the meat is cured in a salt and spice mix (to pickle it) before being boiled. A variety of spices are rubbed onto the meat, and this kills bacteria and draws out moisture, which cures the meat. It needs to be pickled in the fridge for 2 weeks until it is cured. Then it needs to be boiled a few times and simmered until tender. It is delicious, especially when thinly sliced and served with either mustard or horseradish sauce. It's perfect in a sandwich made with rye bread.

Ingredients

- 4 lb (1.8 kg) beef tongue or beef brisket
- ½ cup (120 ml) warm water
- ¼ cup (70 g) kosher salt
- 1 tablespoon brown sugar
- 1 tablespoon saltpeter (potassium nitrate)
- 1 teaspoon whole peppercorns
- 2 teaspoons ground ginger
- ½ teaspoon whole cloves
- ⅛ teaspoon ground nutmeg
- ⅛ teaspoon paprika
- 3 garlic cloves, minced
- 2 bay leaves, crumbled

Instructions

1. Remove the fat from the tongue or brisket.

2. Mix together the salt, spices, sugar, and garlic, and then rub the mixture over the meat. Place it into a non-metal container that will fit in the fridge.

3. Dissolve the saltpeter in warm water and pour over the meat.

4. Weigh the meat down with something heavy, and cover the container with a lid or plastic wrap and keep refrigerated for 14 days, turning the meat every 2 days.

5. Remove the meat from the brine and place in a large pot with cold water. Bring it to a boil. Remove the meat. Discard the water. Do this 3 more times.

6. Next, place the meat in the pot. Cover with cold water again and bring to a boil. Lower the heat, and let the meat simmer for 2 hours or until the meat is tender.

7. Serve with mustard or horseradish sauce.

6. Pickled Sausage

Pickling sausages can help them to keep a little longer in the fridge until you want to use them for meals. It will also combine the tangy flavor of pickle with the savory flavor of sausage. They will keep in the fridge for 7 days after you've pickled them. They are great to snack on as well as a lovely accompaniment to rice, cheese trays, in a casserole, a 5-bean salad, or jambalaya.

Ingredients

- ½ lb (225 g) pork sausages
- 1 cup (240 ml) white vinegar
- 1 cup (240 ml) water
- 2 tablespoons sugar
- 1 tablespoon pickling, pure, kosher, or sea salt
- 2 cloves garlic
- 2 bay leaves
- ¼ teaspoon black peppercorn
- ⅓ teaspoon ground turmeric

Instructions

1. Cook the sausages over a medium heat and allow to cool.
2. Slice the sausages diagonally into pieces—you can use the end pieces of each sausage as snacking sausage.
3. Place the sausage slices in a jar.
4. Add the garlic cloves, peppercorns, bay leaves, and turmeric to the jars.
5. In a saucepan, place the vinegar, water, salt, and sugar and bring to a boil.
6. Once it has boiled, pour the brine over the sausage slices in the jars. Ensure the sausage slices are fully submerged.
7. Put a lid on the jar and put it in the fridge. These will keep up to 7 days there.

7. Pickled Fish

Ingredients

- 4.5 lb (2 kg) firm white fish fillets
- 1 cup (120 g) flour
- Vegetable oil—to fry the fish
- 6 large onions, peeled and sliced
- 1 cup (240 ml) vinegar
- 1 cup (240 ml) filtered water
- 3–4 tablespoons sugar
- 2 tablespoons apricot jam
- 1 tablespoon corn flour mixed with 3 tablespoons water
- 2 tablespoons roasted masala
- 2 teaspoons turmeric
- 1 teaspoon ground black pepper
- 1 tablespoon coriander seeds
- 5 bay leaves
- 1 tablespoon black peppercorns

Instructions

1. Dredge the fish pieces in the flour and season with salt and pepper.
2. In a frying pan, heat the oil, then fry the fish for 2 minutes on each side. Place on draining paper.
3. In a large saucepan, heat the vinegar and water. Add the onions, sugar, salt, spices, jam, and bay leaves and cook for 10 minutes.
4. Add the corn flour mixture into this, and stir well.
5. Next, put the fish, onion, and curry sauce mixture into a large dish, ensuring the sauce covers the fish completely.

6. Allow all this to cool before covering the container and storing in the fridge overnight or for up to a few days.

8. Pickled Pike

When you pickle pike, the vinegar softens the bones to such an extent that they are no longer noticeable. Pickled pike is a Scandinavian/Eastern European version of ceviche. It is lovely on crackers, as a snack, or an appetizer. It goes perfectly with pale ale. Northern pike is what's typically used, but you could use any firm white fish for the recipe. You should freeze the fish for 48 hours before cooking to kill any parasites.

Ingredients

- 1 lb (450 g) pike, cut into ½-inch (1.2 cm) pieces
- 1 red onion, thinly sliced
- 5 cups (1.2 L) water
- 2 cups (480 ml) cider vinegar
- 1 cup (280 g) pickling, pure, kosher, or sea salt
- ⅓ cup (67 g) sugar
- 2 teaspoons black peppercorns
- 2 teaspoons whole allspice
- 1 teaspoon mustard seeds
- 2 bay leaves
- Zest of a lemon

Instructions

1. Heat 4 cups (960 ml) of water and dissolve the salt in it. Let this completely cool.

2. Place the pike pieces in the salty brine overnight.

3. In a saucepan, heat the remaining cup (240 ml) of water, vinegar, sugar, and spices and bring to a boil. Simmer it for 5 minutes, then let it cool.

4. Put the pike in glass jars. Add the lemon zest, bay leaves, and thinly sliced red onion.

5. Pour the pickling liquid over the pike pieces. Seal the jar.

6. Place in the fridge and wait a week before eating. You can store the jar in the fridge for up to a month.

9. Cape Malay Pickled Fish

This recipe originated in Cape Town, South Africa, and it was made at Easter time, where people would serve the pickled fish with hot cross buns or freshly baked bread. This is the perfect thing to eat for lunch with bread and a green salad. This recipe can be made with cod, canned tuna, and yellowfish.

Ingredients

- 3 lb (1.35 kg) cod fillets, cut into 2–3 oz (60–90 g) pieces
- 2 large onions, peeled and sliced into rings
- 1 red chili pepper, seeded and sliced lengthways (if you don't have a red chili pepper, you can use peri-peri or Tabasco sauce)
- 2 cups (480 ml) red wine vinegar (if you find it too acidic, just add 1½ cups (360 ml) of vinegar, or you could always add a little more water, or have a mix of red wine vinegar and white wine vinegar)
- ½ cup (120 ml) water
- ½ cup (100 g) brown sugar
- ½ cup (120 ml) vegetable oil for frying
- Salt to taste
- 2 cloves garlic, chopped
- 2 tablespoons curry powder (you can use fish masala instead of curry powder)
- 2 teaspoons ground cumin
- 2 teaspoons ground coriander

- 1 teaspoon ground turmeric
- 3 large bay leaves
- 4 whole allspice berries
- 8 whole black peppercorns

Instructions

1. Heat the oil in a frying pan. Season the fish with salt and fry until it's golden and flakes with a fork—approximately 5 minutes each side.

2. Add onions and garlic to the pan, and cook them for approximately 5 minutes until they go translucent.

3. Add the chili pepper, bay leaves, peppercorns, allspice berries, and vinegar, and bring the mixture to a boil. Stir in the brown sugar until it has dissolved. Add the curry powder, cumin, coriander, and turmeric. Taste it, and if you want it sweeter, add in more brown sugar.

4. Put the fish into a serving dish, and cover it with the pickling liquid. Keep it at room temperature until it has cooled—this typically takes about 30 minutes. Cover it, and place it in the fridge for 24 hours before serving.

10. Fermented Fish

Another name for this recipe is Gefilte fish. It is traditionally served as an appetizer in Ashkenazi Jewish households in Eastern Europe. If you're not so keen on getting a raw fish taste, then you may want to add more seasoning. This recipe is popular in Poland and Lithuania (but with no sugar and beets included). This particular recipe has more of a Ukrainian feel, with added carrot and parsnip to give it a sweeter taste and a rougher texture.

Ingredients

- 7½ lb (3.4 kg) whole carp, whitefish, and pike, filleted and ground (you can ask your fishmonger to grind the fish but to save you the tails, fins, heads, and bones).
- 3 onions, peeled
- 4 medium carrots, peeled
- 1 small parsnip, chopped
- 4 large eggs
- 1 gallon (3.8L) cold water
- 3 teaspoons salt
- 2 tablespoons sugar
- Freshly ground black pepper
- ⅓ cup matzah meal (also called matzo meal)

Instructions

1. Place the bones, skin, and fish heads in a saucepan, add the water and 2 teaspoons of salt. Bring it to a boil. Keep skimming off the foam that occurs. This will create a fish stock.

2. Cut 1 onion into rounds, and add along with 3 carrots into the fish stock. Add the sugar and bring to a boil. Cover and simmer for 20 minutes.

3. Put the ground fish in a bowl. Use a food processor to chop the remaining onions and carrot, and add the parsnip too. Add the chopped vegetables to the ground fish.

4. Gradually add the eggs, one at a time, plus the salt, pepper, and cold water to the ground fish and chopped vegetables and mix. Stir in enough matzah meal to make a light, soft mixture into oval shapes about 3 inches (7.5 cm) in length.

5. Take out the onions, skins, head, and bones, and let the stock simmer.

6. Put the fish patties into the simmering fish stock and simmer for 30 minutes. Shake the pot from time to time to stop the patties from sticking to one another. Once they are ready, remove the patties from the water, and let them cool for 15 minutes.

7. Arrange the gefilte fish patties onto a platter, strain some of the stock over them, and save the rest in a bowl.

8. Slice the cooked carrots into rounds ¼ inch (6 mm) thick, and put a carrot round on top of each gefilte fish patty.

9. Chill until you are ready to serve. You can put parsley and horseradish on the patties.

11. Easy Pickled Eggs

These pickled eggs make a delicious snack, and they go well with a charcuterie board too. They're also lovely on salads, and in the UK, they're often served as an accompaniment to fish and chips.

Ingredients

- 12 hard-boiled eggs, peeled
- 1 large onion, thinly sliced
- 1 cup (240 ml) water
- 3 cups (720 ml) white vinegar
- ⅓ cup (67 g) sugar
- 1 teaspoon pickling, pure, kosher, or sea salt
- 2–3 sprigs dill
- 1 bay leaf
- 1 clove garlic
- 4 teaspoons pickling spice

Instructions

1. Slice the onion into thin slices, then place the onion, white vinegar, salt, sugar, bay leaf, and pickling spice in a saucepan. Bring the mixture to a boil, and turn the heat down to a simmer for 5 minutes. Let this cool.

2. Put a garlic clove in a glass jar, and put 3 hard boiled eggs on top.

3. Next, place some of the onion mixture and a sprig of fresh dill on top.

4. Continue layering eggs and the onion and dill mixture until the jar is full.

5. Pour the pickling liquid over the eggs, onions, and dill.

6. Put a lid on the jar and place in the fridge for a week before consuming.

12. Spicy Fermented Eggs

Fermented eggs have a pickled twang to them, but they're not quite as strong as pickled eggs. If you want a snack rich in protein or something to accompany a salad, a spicy fermented egg can be perfect.

Ingredients

- 15 hard-boiled chicken eggs (or you could use 30 quail eggs), peeled
- ½ jalapeno pepper
- 1 cup (240 ml) filtered water
- 1 tablespoon pickling, pure, kosher, or sea salt
- ½ teaspoon starter culture or ¼ cup (60 ml) whey
- 2 sprigs fresh dill
- 2 cloves garlic
- ⅛ teaspoon whole peppercorns

Instructions

1. Put the starter culture or whey and the salt into the water and stir to ensure it is all dissolved.

2. Peel your eggs, and put them in a jar with the peppercorns, sprigs of dill, garlic, and jalapeno pepper.

3. Pour the brine over the eggs, ensuring they are fully submerged (use a weight to keep them under the brine).

4. Put a lid on the jar, and leave these at room temperature for 3 days. Remember to burp the jar daily if you don't have a fermentation lid with an airlock. Then you can place them in a fridge, and they will keep there for 2 weeks.

13. Beet Pickled Eggs with Cardamom and Anise

These lovely looking eggs really make a statement on the dinner table or for picnics, and they taste amazing too. The longer you pickle them, the pinker they turn. Even the yolk will eventually turn pink if pickled for long enough. They are great for snacks or for salads, and you can put them on sandwiches and in wraps or on top of avocado toast.

Ingredients

- 6 hard-boiled eggs, peeled
- 1 beet, peeled and chopped into 1–2-inch (2.5–5 cm) pieces
- ¼ onion, sliced into rings
- 1 cup (240 ml) beet juice
- 1 cup (240 ml) apple cider vinegar
- ⅓ cup (67 g) sugar
- 1 star anise
- 3 cardamom pods

Instructions

1. Boil the eggs and peel them.
2. Place the eggs into a quart (0.95L) glass jar.
3. Put the vinegar, water, beet, beet juice, onion, sugar, and spices in a saucepan and bring to a boil. Let the sugar dissolve. The onions should be translucent. Turn the heat down and simmer for 5 minutes. Remove from heat and let it cool.

4. Pour the vinegar mixture over the eggs, ensuring they are completely submerged. Ensure that the cooked beets are in the jar too to add color to the eggs.

5. Seal the jar and refrigerate for 3 days.

6. You can eat the eggs after 3 days, and they'll keep in the fridge for up to a month. The longer they pickle, the pinker they will become.

14. Curried Pickled Eggs

These vibrant, spiced pickled eggs melt delicate curry spices with tangy pickle. You can make them ahead and store them in the fridge for up to a month, so you've always got a quick and healthy snack. They also work great as a bar snack with an ice-cold beer.

Ingredients

- 6 hard-boiled eggs, peeled
- ¼ onion, sliced
- 1 cup (240 ml) apple cider vinegar
- ¾ cup (180 ml) water
- ¾ cup (150 g) sugar
- 1 tablespoon yellow curry powder
- 1 teaspoon mustard seeds
- 3 cardamom pods

Instructions

1. Boil the eggs, and peel them.
2. Place the eggs into a quart (0.95L) glass jar
3. Put the vinegar, water, yellow curry powder, mustard seeds, onion, sugar, and spices in a saucepan and bring to a boil. Let the sugar dissolve. The onions should be translucent. Turn the heat down

and simmer for 5 minutes. Remove from heat and let it cool.

4. Pour the vinegar mixture over the eggs, ensuring they are completely submerged. Ensure that the mustard seeds and cardamom pods are in the jar too.

5. Seal the jar and refrigerate for 3 days.

6. You can eat the eggs after 3 days, and they'll keep in the fridge for up to a month. The longer they pickle, the more yellow they will become from the curry powder.

15. Red Vinegar Pickled Eggs

These are really unusual looking pickled eggs, and they have a delicious taste. This is an Italian recipe from Tuscany. The eggs look stunning sliced for salads, in sandwiches, or on charcutier or cheese boards.

Ingredients

- 12 hard-boiled eggs, peeled
- 1 pepperoncino
- 4 cups (960 ml) red vinegar
- 1 tablespoon pickling, pure, kosher, or sea salt
- 5 cloves garlic, in their skins
- 5 bay leaves
- 20 black peppercorns

Instructions

1. Hard-boil your eggs. Usually boiling them in a saucepan for 10 minutes should suffice. Place them in cold water after cooking to stop the yolks from discoloring. Peel the eggs.

2. Put the vinegar, garlic, black peppercorns, bay leaves, pepperoncino, and salt in a saucepan. Bring it to a boil. Then simmer it for 5 minutes. Let the liquid cool.

3. Place the eggs in a glass jar. Pour the brine over the eggs.

4. Seal the jar. Keep it closed for 1 month before eating the eggs.

5. The eggs will become a deep chestnut color.

One of my favorite things to pickle from this chapter is the beet pickled eggs just because of how stunningly vivid they look. They are a really unique dish for dinner parties, with the vibrant pink outside, a small bit of white, and the bright yellow yolks. They are guaranteed to get comments from your friends and family, and they taste great too. I do also love the curried eggs—they are a great nighttime snack when you fancy something savory.

Key takeaways from this chapter:

1. Pickled meat usually needs to be boiled after pickling before you can eat it.

2. Pickling sausages helps preserve them—they will keep in the fridge for 7 days after pickling.

3. When pickling corned beef, use pink salt (that contains nitrates) to stop the cooked beef from becoming grey.

4. Always remember that you can add different spices to suit your taste when pickling.

5. Remember to place boiled/steamed eggs under cold running water to stop the yolk from looking grey.

6. Remember to freeze pike or white fish before you pickle it to kill parasites.

The next chapter will focus on non-alcoholic fermented drinks, including kombucha tea, kefir, and kvass, among many other recipes for fermented and probiotic drinks, which have incredible health properties, including improving gut health and boosting your immune system.

Chapter 9: Fermented Beverages

This chapter is about fermented beverages, and they are one of my favorite things to make because they're so refreshing, taste delicious, and are good for your health. There's a wide variety of fermented drinks that you can make. I love the fact that when you make your own, you know exactly what has gone into it. You can make use of the plants, fruits, and spices that you grow in your own garden. When you buy fermented drinks from a shop, they are super expensive, so this is another good reason to make your own. This chapter gives you recipes and instructions for how to make kombucha, switchel, punch, kvass, root beer, ginger ale, fermented lemonade, tepache, kefir, fermented sodas, and more.

Fermented Beverages Recipes

1. Homemade Kombucha

Kombucha is a fermented drink from culturing sweetened black tea with a symbiotic culture of bacteria and yeast (known as SCOBY). If you've ever seen someone brew kombucha at home, the SCOBY is a pellicle that forms on top of the brew (you can see it in the picture below).

The SCOBY is the "mother" that kick-starts each batch of kombucha, while also protecting the kombucha from contaminants, like dust and debris. While you can buy a ready-made SCOBY, it's easy to make it yourself. The SCOBY converts the sugar in sweet tea into B vitamins and acids, creating kombucha. Making kombucha involves 3 major steps:

- Make SCOBY (1–4 weeks)—to make the "mother".

- First fermentation (6–10 days)—to make actual kombucha

- Second fermentation (3 to 10 days)—to carbonate the kombucha

Making SCOBY
Ingredients

- 7 cups (1.68L) filtered water (tap water should be fine after boiling it for 15 minutes and letting it sit for 24 hours in an open container)

- ½ cup (100 g) white sugar (Using simple, plain white sugar made from either cane or beets is best. Raw or whole cane sugar will work too, but it can be hard on your SCOBY. Do not use honey (it may contain botulism bacteria), brown sugar (molasses in it can harm SCOBY), powdered sugar (it contains cornstarch), agave, maple, coconut, or palm sugar (these can be hard on SCOBY and cause the kombucha have an odd flavor), or any sugar substitutes (because bacteria need actual sugar to work).)

- 4 bags black tea or 1 tablespoon loose tea, which I personally prefer (Use only black tea when growing SCOBY. Do not use decaf tea because SCOBY will got grow well. Similarly, it won't grow well if you use green or fruit teas.)

- 1 cup (240 ml) unpasteurized, unflavored store-bought kombucha

- A large glass or ceramic container (A jug holding at least 1 gallon (3.8 L) or 2 jars holding at least ½ gallon (1.9 L) each. Do not use metal or plastic containers because metals can react with the acidic kombucha and hurt your SCOBY, while plastic can house nasty bacteria that you obviously don't want in your kombucha.)

- Tightly woven cloth (coffee filters, paper towels, napkins, cheesecloth)

- Rubber bands

Instructions

1. Bring the water to a boil in a clean pot. Remove from heat and add the sugar.

2. Add the tea and allow to steep while the water cools to room temperature (which will usually take a few hours). The water is ready to work with only when it's at room temperature because hot water will kill the SCOBY.

3. Pour the sweetened tea into your jars, then add the store-bought kombucha (if you're using 2 jars, pour half of the starter kombucha into each), making sure to include any little pieces of gunk that may be at the bottom—these are good.

4. Cover with a few layers of tightly woven cloth (this will help keep out bugs and debris) and secure with a rubber band.

5. Set in a place where it's dark, still, and the temperature is around 70–75°F (21–24°C), like a

cupboard, for 1–4 weeks until a ¼-inch (6 mm) SCOBY has formed.

6. Keep SCOBY in its original tea until you're ready to brew your first batch of kombucha. The SCOBY can live and grow for years if treated right. The tea you used to make the SCOBY will become very vinegary and should be tossed. Don't use this tea as the starter to your first fermentation.

First Fermentation

So, you've made a SCOBY, and now you're ready to make your own homemade kombucha. This first fermentation is where you actually make the kombucha.

Ingredients

- 14 cups (3.36L) filtered water (tap water should be fine after boiling it for 15 minutes and letting it sit for 24 hours in an open container)

- 1 cup (200 g) white sugar

- 8 bags black or green tea or 2 tablespoons loose leaf tea (Unlike when making SCOBY, you can use other teas besides black for first fermentation. Feel free to experiment with green, white, oolong, or different combinations of teas. Fruit teas should be mixed with a few black tea bags to ensure the SCOBY "mother" gets what she needs to thrive.)

- 2 cups (480 ml) unflavored kombucha (either from a previous batch or unpasteurized, unflavored store-bought kombucha)

- 1 or 2 SCOBYs (depending on how many containers you're using—1 per container)

- A large glass or ceramic container (A jug holding at least 1 gallon (3.8 L) or 2 jars holding at least ½ gallon (1.9 L) each. Do not use metal or plastic containers because metals can react with the acidic kombucha and hurt your SCOBY, while plastic can house nasty bacteria that you obviously don't want in your kombucha)

- Tightly woven cloth (coffee filters, paper towels, napkins, cheese cloth)
- Rubber bands

Instructions

1. Bring the water to a boil in a clean pot. Remove from heat and add the sugar.

2. Add the tea and allow to steep while the water cools to room temperature (which will usually take a few hours). Again, the water is ready to work with only when it's at room temperature because hot water can kill the SCOBY.

3. Wash your hands thoroughly, and gently remove your SCOBY from the tea and place it on a clean plate. You can rinse out the jar if you want (without soap), but it's not necessary.

4. Pour the sweetened tea into your jar(s), then pour in the unflavored starter kombucha (if you're using 2 jars, pour half of the starter kombucha into each).

5. Gently place 1 SCOBY into each jar, then cover with a few layers of the tightly woven cloth and secure with a rubber band.

6. Set in a place where it's dark, still, and the temperature is around 70–75°F (21–24°C) for anywhere from 6 to 10 days. You can start tasting the tea after 6 days by gently drawing out some of the tea with a paper straw. Use your finger to hold the tea in the straw—don't use your mouth. It should be mildly sweet and slightly vinegary. The warmer the room temperature, the faster the kombucha will ferment. The longer the tea ferments, the more sugar molecules will be eaten up, and the less sweet it will become.

7. Reserve 2 cups from this batch to use as starter kombucha for your next batch (you can just leave it in the jar with SCOBYs). The rest can move into the second and final fermentation.

Second Fermentation

Second fermentation is the final step in making homemade kombucha, and it's perhaps the best part of the process. The second fermentation is where the real magic happens. This is where you can play around with different flavors as well as carbonate your kombucha into effervescent bliss.

Ingredients

- Homemade kombucha from the first fermentation
- Sweetener (fruits, honey, or sugar).
- There are a lot of different flavors you can go for, but typically you would add 1–2 tablespoons of mashed fruit or fruit juice and 1–2 teaspoons of honey or sugar per cup (240 ml) of kombucha.
- My personal favorite recipe is lemon ginger kombucha. For this, you will need ¼ cup (60 ml)

lemon juice, 1 tablespoon of chopped or grated ginger, and 2 teaspoons of honey for ½ gallon (1.9L) of kombucha.

- Another great recipe I absolutely adore is orange and vanilla kombucha, which tastes like orange creamsicle—it's absolutely delicious. You will need ½ cup (120 ml) of orange juice and ½ teaspoon vanilla extract for ½ gallon (1.9L) of kombucha.

- A few flip top fermentation bottles (Bottles meant for fermentation have an airtight seal, which will prevent carbonation from escaping. If you don't have these, canning jars will do the job, although they aren't truly airtight.)

Instructions

1. Strain the kombucha and funnel into bottles, leaving about 1½ inches (3.8 cm) of space at the top.

2. Add your chosen sweetener, and seal the lid tightly.

3. Let the bottles ferment in a place where it's dark, still, and the temperature is around 70–75°F (21–24°C) for anywhere between 3 and 10 days.

4. You can strain out fruit before serving if you want. Place the kombucha in the fridge to slow the carbonation process.

2. Continuous Brew Kombucha

Once you have made some homemade kombucha, you can keep brewing it for as long as you like. This continuous brew kombucha is much cheaper than buying it from stores, and you can really experiment with different flavors. This technique uses a larger vessel with a spigot so that you can release the amount of kombucha you want when you need it rather than

having to use it all at once. Many people start with 2 gallons (7.8L). When it has finished brewing and produces a baby SCOBY, you can draw off ⅓ of the kombucha, replace that with fresh sweet tea, and it will just keep on producing indefinitely. Continuous brew ferments faster than when making kombucha from scratch. It allows you to make a decent volume at once, which is ideal for families (or if you simply drink a lot of it). There's also less chance of contamination from mold or microbes.

Ingredients

- Kombucha "mother" or SCOBY

- ¼ cup (28 grams) loose leaf black tea (ideally) but you can use green, oolong, or other types of tea

- 2 cups (400 g) sugar

- 2 cups (480 ml) starter kombucha tea from the first fermentation (see previous recipe), or you can use store-bought unflavored, unpasteurized kombucha

Instructions

1. Your continuous brew container should hold between 2 and 5 gallons (7.8–19L), and it should also have a spigot for drawing off the tea. The spigot should be plastic, wooden, or stainless steel. Ideally, the spigot should be in the center of the container rather than at the bottom (if you can't find a container with a spigot in the center, stir the kombucha before drawing any off). Stirring it for optimal microbial balance is always a good idea before removing kombucha.

2. Bring 2 quarts (1.9L) of water to a boil. Turn off the heat, and stir in the tea and sugar. Stir until the sugar has dissolved. Allow the tea to sit and cool to room temperature.

3. Strain the tea through a fine mesh sieve into the continuous brew container.

4. Add the kombucha mother and the starter kombucha tea to the container.

5. Cover it loosely, and allow it to ferment for a week or until you see a new mother forming.

6. After a week, draw off up to a ¼ of kombucha, bottle it, and replace that same amount with sweet tea. After this week, you can draw off kombucha as often as you like—typically 1–3 times a week—and replace it with the equivalent of sweet tea.

7. When you have drawn off the kombucha, place it in a flip top bottle. You can flavor it by adding 1–2 tablespoons of mashed fruit or fruit juice and 1–2 teaspoons of honey or sugar per cup (240 ml) of kombucha.

8. Close the bottle. Allow it to ferment for a further 3–10 days, then place it in the fridge and drink whenever you like.

Useful Tips

- Keep at least 20% of the kombucha in there so that there is plenty of bacteria and yeast to ferment the sweet tea.

- Always replace what you drew off.

- You may need to separate SCOBY layers (you can give extras that grow to friends or compost them).

- Keep the spigot clean from yeast or SCOBY.

3. Haymaker's Punch

This is a drink that tastes both sweet and sour, with some fiery ginger kick to it also. It's a refreshing drink, ideal on hot days. In the past, farmers used to drink it when they harvested their hay, which has given the drink its name. It would rehydrate them and give them energy. This drink is also sometimes called switchel or ginger water, and it was popular with sailors too. In the 19th century, ships would stock the ingredients for this drink ready for long journeys. The drink is good for your health because the cider vinegar in it helps your metabolism and blood sugar, the electrolytes hydrate you and help the cells in your body, the molasses contains vitamin B6, which is good for your heart and brain, and the ginger is anti-inflammatory. When you serve it, it's best served over ice. You could add some sparkling water to give it a ginger ale feel.

Ingredients

- 8 cups (1.92L) warm water

- ¼ teaspoon fine sea salt

- ¼ cup (60 ml) molasses

- ¼ cup (60 ml) raw apple cider vinegar
- 2 teaspoons ground ginger

Instructions

1. The instructions could not be simpler—you simply need to whisk all the ingredients together and then refrigerate it. You need to shake it thoroughly before serving. It will keep in the fridge for up to 5 days.

4. Blackberry Switchel

This is a beautiful, vibrant looking drink. It is essentially a variation of the haymaker's punch recipe above. It smells and tastes amazing, has an excellent sounding name, and is a lovely drink that will keep you well hydrated—it's so nice to have it over ice on a hot day. It's also called switzel, swizzle, haymaker's punch, and sometimes ginger water. It's a drink that originated in the 18th century in colonial America. Farmers and sailors drank this to quench their thirst after working hard. It's a natural version of sports drinks today. Making a switchel is a great way to use up any overripe or an abundance of fruit. This particular recipe has blackberry and ginger in it, and it will give you a natural source of electrolytes. Switchel contains four basic ingredients: vinegar, water, ginger, and a sweetener. Some recipes also include fruit, typically berries or stone fruits, such as peaches and plums. This recipe includes blackberries, and it's absolutely delicious!

Ingredients

- 2 cups (300 g) blackberries
- 8 cups (1.92L) water
- ¼ cup (60 ml) apple cider vinegar
- ¼ cup (85 g) honey

- 3-inch (7.5 cm) knob fresh ginger, peeled and chopped
- Pinch fine sea salt

Instructions

1. Put the ingredients in a saucepan and bring to a boil. Then reduce the heat and simmer for 15 minutes. Mash the softened berries into the liquid and simmer for a further 5 minutes after that.
2. Strain the switchel, discard the solids, refrigerate overnight, and then serve cold over ice.

Useful Tips

Initially when this was made, molasses would have been used to sweeten the drink, so you could try it with molasses as well as brown sugar or maple syrup. You could also change the type of berries used and try raspberries or loganberries. You could add some lemon juice too.

5. Traditional Bread Kvass

Kvass is one of my favorite drinks ever! It's so lovely and refreshing on a hot summer day. Kvass is a traditional Eastern European fermented drink, which is typically made with stale, toasted sourdough rye bread. While bread kvass is the most popular, other versions exist, including those made with beets and fruits. It tastes of honey and malt, similar to a cross between a blonde beer and mead. However, it contains much less alcohol than those drinks. Due to its rather short fermentation cycle, it usually contains as much alcohol as other similar drinks, such as kombucha or kefir, ranging from 0.3 to 1.5%.

Ingredients

- 2½ gallons (9.5L) water

- 1 lb (450 g) or 9 slices classic black, dark, or rye bread
- 1 handful raisins
- 4 cups (800 g) sugar
- 1½ tablespoons active dry yeast
- 3 large plastic soda bottles

Instructions

1. Fill a giant stockpot with 2½ gallons of water (or divide it into 2 large pots) and bring to a boil.

2. While waiting, toast the bread slices twice on the darkest toaster setting. Yes, that's right. Darker bread makes darker, stronger kvass. You can also toast the bread in the oven (at 350°F (180°C) for 20 minutes or longer if required) or on a frying pan.

3. When water starts to boil, remove the pot from the heat. Add a handful of raisins and toasted bread to the pot, cover with the lid, and let it stay overnight or at least for 8 hours.

4. Carefully remove the toasted bread and discard it.

5. In a medium bowl, mix together the sugar and yeast, add them to kvass mixture, and stir.

6. Cover with plastic wrap or a lid and leave the mixture on the counter for another 6 hours, stirring every couple of hours.

7. Discard floating raisins by scooping them up with a large spoon. Using a strainer or a cheesecloth, pour the kvass into bottles, loosely cover with lid, and refrigerate overnight. The following day, once the bottles are completely chilled, you can tighten the lid. That's it, your homemade kvass is ready. Enjoy!

6. Fruit Kvass

While I personally prefer traditional bread kvass, this is a nice variation that has a subtle fizz to it and lovely sweetness from the berries. It is delicious and refreshing.

Ingredients

- 1 cup (166 g) strawberries, hulled and quartered
- 1 cup (130 g) raspberries
- ½ cup (95 g) blueberries
- 4 cups (960 ml) water
- 2 tablespoons honey
- ½ teaspoon fine sea salt

Instructions

1. Place the strawberries and raspberries into a quart (0.95L) jar.

2. Whisk the water, honey, and salt and pour over the berries, leaving 1 inch (2.5 cm) of space at the top of the jar.

3. Seal the jar tightly, and then shake it.

4. Let the fruit kvass ferment at room temperature for 3 days. Shake the jar each day, and burp it twice a day. When you open the jar to burp it and it hisses when you open it, you know that it is ready.

5. Strain the kvass using a fine mesh sieve, and discard the fruit.

6. Place it into a clean bottle and either drink immediately, or it will keep in the fridge for up to 1 week.

7. Orange Ginger Carrot Kvass

To be perfectly honest, when I first came across this recipe, I was a bit skeptical. As mentioned previously, I prefer traditional bread kvass, and this just seemed a bit odd. But I do love oranges and carrots, so I decided to give it a try, and I'm so glad I did! It is tangy, aromatic, and so pleasant to drink. Give it a try, you won't regret it!

Ingredients

- 6 carrots, sliced in 1/8-inch (3 mm) circles
- 6 large strips organic orange peel
- 2 tablespoons ginger, roughly chopped
- 2 tablespoons sea salt
- ¼ cup (60 ml) whey
- Filtered water

Instructions

1. Place the carrots, ginger, and orange peel into a half-gallon (1.9L) jar.
2. Add the whey and salt, and fill up the jar with water, ensuring you leave 1 inch (2.5 cm) of space at the top.
3. Place a lid on the jar, and shake it to dissolve the salt and whey.
4. Remove the lid and cover with either a clean towel or a coffee filter, and secure this with a rubber band or a canning ring.
5. Place the jar in a warm spot, and allow it to ferment for 4 days.
6. You can strain most of the liquid from the carrots, orange, and ginger, leaving just 1 cup (240 ml) of liquid in the jar so that you can make another round of kvass should you want to. If you decide to make a second, weaker batch of kvass, then add water and repeat the fermentation steps above.

8. Homemade Root Beer

Root beer has a very distinctive, homely, almost medicinal/botanical taste. The origins of root beer can be traced back to 18th century American farm brewers who adapted native North American recipes to make very low or non-alcoholic family drinks. Root beer naturally has bubbles because it's fermented. It's nice to make the recipe closer to the original way rather than the store-bought carbonated options of today. You will need some ginger bug, which is a wild-fermented starter culture, to kick-start the fermentation process. You can either buy it or make your own. If you don't have a ginger bug starter culture, you could use kombucha, jun tea, or water kefir instead.

Making Ginger Bug

Ingredients

To Start the Bug

- 2 cups (480 ml) water
- 2 teaspoons sugar
- 1 oz (30 g) fresh ginger, diced

To Feed the Bug

- 5 teaspoons sugar
- 2½ oz (75 g) fresh ginger, diced

To Use the Bug

- 8 cups (1.92L) fruit juice or sweetened herbal tea

Instructions

Preparing the Bug

1. Warm the water in a saucepan over medium heat, and stir in the sugar until it has fully dissolved. Let this cool to room temperature.

2. Drop the ginger into a pint-sized (473 ml) jar, and then cover it with the sugar water. Seal the jar, and let it culture at room temperature for 1 day.

Feeding the Bug

3. The next day, and each day for 5 days, stir 1 teaspoon of sugar and ½ an ounce (15 g) of ginger into the jar, and then close the jar tightly. Between 3 and 5 days, you should start to see bubbles forming, and your bug should smell yeasty and gingery. When you see bubbles, your bug is ready to use.

Using the Bug

4. To use the bug, strain ½ a cup (120 ml) of the liquid, and mix it with 7½ cups (1.8L) of liquid such as fruit juice or sweetened herbal tea, bottle it, and ferment up to 3 days.

Making Root Beer

Ingredients

- 10 cups (2.4L) water
- ¾ cup (150 g) unrefined cane sugar (you can also use maple syrup, honey, or coconut sugar)
- ½ cup (120 ml) ginger bug
- ¼ cup (28 g) sassafras root bark
- 3 tablespoons sarsaparilla root
- 2 teaspoons birch bark
- 2 teaspoons dandelion root (you can use mint instead if you like)
- 1 tablespoon ginger root
- 1 tablespoon licorice root
- 1 star anise

Instructions

1. Place the water in a large stockpot. Add in the sarsaparilla root, star anise, licorice, birch bark, ginger root, and dandelion.

2. Bring it to a boil, and then turn down the heat and simmer for 30 minutes. Add in the sassafras bark and simmer for another 15 minutes.

3. Take the pot off the heat, and stir in the sugar until it has completely dissolved. Let this cool for approximately 2 hours.

4. Strain the liquid, and discard the herbs.

5. Stir in the ginger bug.

6. Pour the liquid into flip top bottles. Leave 1½ inches (3.8 cm) of space at the top of each bottle.

7. Let the root beer ferment at room temperature for 2 days (if you live somewhere very cold, it may need a bit longer). Then place in the fridge for 3 days to allow the bubbles to settle.

8. You can then serve this over ice.

9. Homemade Ginger Ale

This natural, homemade ginger ale is so much healthier than store-bought alternatives that are filled with sugars and preservatives. It's a fermented drink that replenishes your microbiome, giving you good bacteria in your digestive system, which helps you to absorb nutrients, have a healthy colon, and boosts your immune system. You will need a ginger bug to start this fermentation—making it was covered in the previous recipe. If you don't have that or can't or don't want to make it, you could replace it with ⅛ teaspoon of active yeast. The sugar in this recipe is to feed the bacteria and get the drink to be fizzy.

Ingredients

- 6 cups (1.44L) purified water
- ½ cup (100 g) white sugar
- ½ cup (120 ml) ginger bug (or ⅛ teaspoon active yeast)
- 1 lemon, peeled and sliced
- 2 inches (5 cm) ginger root, peeled and grated

Instructions

1. In a stockpot or a large saucepan, add 4 cups (960 ml) of water, grated ginger, and sugar, and bring it to a boil.
2. Turn the heat down, and simmer it for 5 minutes. Then strain the liquid, discard any solids, and let the liquid cool.
3. Put the cooled mixture in a jar, add the rest of the water as well as the lemon and ginger bug, and stir.
4. Put a tight lid on the jar.
5. Leave on a kitchen surface at room temperature for 3 days. It should be fizzy after this time. Then either drink it immediately, or keep it in the fridge for up to a week.

10. Probiotic Lacto-Fermented Lemonade

Fermentation is wonderful for providing good bacteria for your gut and digestive system. This lacto-fermented lemonade is great to save you money on buying fermented probiotic drinks, which are often not cheap to buy. It will also help you restore your natural bacteria in your gut and improve your overall health. There are many things in life that can disrupt your gut health, so drinking drinks like this will do you the world of good. This recipe produces a tangy, slightly sparkling drink. It's not like a carbonated drink—it's more subtle. It has a slightly sweet taste. It is important to only use fresh lemon juice for this recipe because if you use bottled lemon juice, it may contain preservatives that would stop the fermentation process.

Ingredients

- 6½ cups (1.56L) filtered water
- ½ cup (120 ml) organic freshly squeezed lemon juice
- ½ cup (120 ml) liquid whey
- ½ cup (100 g) organic evaporated cane sugar

Instructions

1. Put the ingredients in a glass jar with a tight-fitting lid.
2. Shake it thoroughly to help the sugar to dissolve.
3. Let this ferment for 2 days at room temperature. Chill the lemonade in the fridge before serving. It will keep up to 10 days in the fridge and will become fizzier with time.

11. Gingered Tepache

This is a Mexican fermented drink that contains pineapple. It's also sometimes called pineapple beer, even though it has no alcohol; however, it's often mixed with rum and pina colada. It also has ginger in it, which gives it some fiery heat that is delicious. This recipe creates a sweet, spicy, and tart pineapple drink that is slightly fizzy and great for your health. Originally, the drink would have been made from pineapple rind, juice, and have cinnamon in it. This fermented drink will hydrate you, help your body cells, replenish your microbiome, and boost your immune system. Pineapple is great as an anti-inflammatory, it heals your digestive system, and it also contains vitamins C and B as well as manganese and copper.

Ingredients

- 1 large ripe pineapple
- 4 cups (960 ml) purified water
- 4 tablespoons Manuka honey (Originally, cane sugar would be used, and it would activate the fermentation in this recipe. This one uses Manuka honey because it has excellent enzymes and healing properties. If you don't have Manuka honey (which can be more expensive), regular honey is fine to use also.)
- 1 inch (2.5 cm) ginger knob, peeled and grated
- 2 cinnamon sticks
- 3 whole cloves

Instructions

1. Peel the pineapple, and place the peel into a large glass jar.
2. Juice the pulp of the pineapple, and pour this over the peel.
3. Mix the water with honey.
4. Add the spices to the honey and water, and pour this into the jar containing the pineapple peel and juiced pulp.
5. Place a small plate on top of the jar, and leave it at room temperate for 3 days.
6. Remove the foam from the top of the jar, cover it again, and let it ferment for 1 more day.
7. Strain the juice, and discard the rind, pulp, and spices.
8. Chill the drink in the fridge before serving.

12. Peaches and Cream Soda

This is a lovely, summery drink that encapsulates the flavors of peaches and cream. This soda is lovely to drink on a hot summer day—it's bubbly, crisp, and delicious. It's not overly sweet because the good bacteria in it use up most of the sugar during the fermentation process.

Ingredients

- 5 cups (750 g) peaches, sliced
- 6 cups (1.44L) water
- 1 cup (200 g) cane sugar
- ½ cup (120 ml) whey
- 2 tablespoons vanilla extract

Instructions

1. Put the peach slices, sugar, and water into a large pot, and bring it to a boil. Reduce it to a simmer for 20 minutes.

2. Use a potato masher to crush the peaches in the pot.

3. Pour the mixture through a fine mesh strainer into a large bowl.

4. Add the vanilla extract and whey to the mixture and stir.

5. Pour this into flip top bottles and leave in a warm area.

6. After 2 days, you can open a bottle and check. You can let the fermented gasses out, and it may take between 2 and 7 days to have the desired fizziness and taste.

7. You can place the bottles in the fridge once they're ready.

13. Ginger Turmeric Water Kefir

Kefir doesn't always have to be thick and yogurt-like. It can be made with water or coconut water, and it's like kombucha but not as tangy. This is a nice, easy recipe to make, and once you've made it, you may wonder why you haven't done so years ago instead of purchasing fermented drinks.

Ingredients

- 3 cups (720 ml) raw coconut water
- ½ cup (120 ml) freshly squeezed orange juice
- 1 packet water kefir starter
- 1 tablespoon turmeric root, peeled and freshly grated (or 1½ teaspoons ground turmeric)
- 1 tablespoon ginger root, peeled and freshly grated

Instructions

1. Put the coconut water and orange juice in a saucepan, and heat them gently until they're lukewarm.

2. Put the lukewarm coconut water and orange juice in a jar, and add the contents of the water kefir starter packet.

3. Add the grated ginger and turmeric. Stir well.

4. Put the lid on the jar.

5. Let the mixture ferment at room temperature for 24 hours.

6. You can taste test it after this time. If you want a tangier drink, then you can leave it for a further 24 hours.

7. When you're happy with the flavor, you can strain the liquid, dispose of the solids, and bottle the liquid in a clean bottle.

8. You can store the kefir in the fridge for up to 3 weeks.

14. Elderflower Soda

This is a spring recipe that I and my whole family love. Elderflower has such a unique, fruity scent. This soda is delicious and easy to make.

Ingredients

- 5 cups (250 g) elderflowers
- ½ gallon (1.9L) filtered water
- ½ cup (100 g) sugar, or ½ cup (170 g) local raw honey, or ½ cup (120 ml) evaporated cane juice
- ¼ cup (60 ml) whey
- Juice of 1 lemon

Instructions

1. Rinse the elderflowers.

2. Put the rinsed elderflowers in a bowl. Heat some filtered water, and pour it over the flowers to cover them entirely. Cover this bowl with a tea towel, and leave them to steep for 48 hours.

3. After this time, strain out the flowers so that you're left with a nice elderflower tea.

4. Add the juice of 1 lemon.

5. Add in a sweetener. The sugar you add will be digested by the good bacteria. You may need to add a little more sweetener, but that will depend on personal taste. We like ours barely sweet.

6. Pour this liquid into a glass container, and add in a couple of tablespoons of whey. Loosely cover it, and place it in a cupboard.

7. It will ferment in 1–2 weeks, but when it's bubbly, you can taste it to see if it's fizzy. If not, let it ferment another couple of days, and then try it again. If you like it, you can put it into flip top bottles and let it sit on the kitchen counter for a further 2 days.

8. Be careful when you open the bottles—you may need to release some gas from the bottle.

9. The bottles will keep in the fridge for up to a week.

15. Fermented Grape Drink

This is a delicious drink that you can enjoy after a few days. It's definitely worth the wait.

Ingredients

- 8 lb (3.6 kg) grapes (you can mix red and green grapes if you wish)
- ¼ cup (60 ml) whey
- ½ tablespoon salt

Instructions

1. Wash the grapes, and remove the stems.

2. Put the grapes through a juicer. Discard the pulp. This should give you about 2 quarts (1.9 L) of grape juice.

3. Add the salt to the grape juice. Mix this well, cover with a tea cloth and a rubber band, and leave on a work surface at room temperature for 3 days.

4. You can check on it from time to time and remove any foam from the surface (you could do this at the start and the end of the day).

5. After 3 days, run the fermented grape juice through a fine mesh strainer.

6. Pour the drink into clean jars, and keep them in the fridge.

7. You can serve the drink with 50% fermented grape juice and 50% mineral water. You can drink this after 3 days, or you can let the bottles remain in the fridge for 2 weeks to give a full grape flavor.

16. Strawberry Kefir Smoothie

These are wonderful to have for breakfast, or as a nice cooling drink on a summer day, or after some sport. For this recipe, you need milk kefir. You can buy kefir from a supermarket, but it's easy to make your own. Simply buy some kefir grains, and add a teaspoon for every cup (240 ml) of milk—when you put the kefir grains into milk, they will digest the milk and turn it into kefir. It's a great source of good bacteria. Generally, it takes about 24–48 hours to turn milk into kefir. It's a hit with all the family, young and old, and you know you're giving your family a good boost of probiotics, fruit, and milk!

Ingredients

- 3 cups (720 ml) milk kefir
- ¾ cup (120 g) frozen strawberries
- ¼ teaspoon stevia powder or honey
- ½ teaspoon almond or vanilla extract

Instructions

1. It's very simple—just place all the ingredients in a blender, and blend until there are no chunks of strawberries remaining. Pour into glasses and drink immediately.

One of my favorite things to make from this chapter is definitely the blackberry switchel. We have lots of blackberry bushes in one corner of our homestead, and in late summer or early fall, we take a container and fill it up with ripe blackberries. We leave them soaking overnight to ensure we get them clean and free from bugs, and then make this delicious, vibrant drink. It's so easy to make and uses natural ingredients that are good for you! It's so tasty and refreshing and gives us a real boost of energy. All our friends love it too.

We also save any scraps of bread and crusts in a Ziplock bag until we have enough to make some bread kvass. Dark rye bread is my personal favorite to give some nice caramel notes to kvass. It's a great way to cut down on food waste and make a delicious drink.

Key takeaways from this chapter:

1. To make kombucha, you need a symbiotic culture of bacteria and yeast, also known as SCOBY.
2. With fermented drinks, remember to burp the jars. When the bottle of a drink hisses when you open it, it's suitably fizzy.
3. Root beer and ginger ale are made using a ginger bug. It's made from sugar, ginger, and water. If you don't have a ginger bug, you can use kombucha, jun tea, or water kefir.
4. Flip top bottles are great for fermented drinks—they are safe and won't explode.

The next chapter will focus on brewing alcohol, and this includes a lovely ginger wine, berry mead, maple mead, pineapple beer, alcoholic ginger beer, and apple cider, among others.

Chapter 10: Brewing Alcohol

This chapter contains recipes and instructions for how you can make fermented alcoholic drinks, such as wine, mead, cider, beer, and pulque. The recipes are varied and delicious. You could make a batch of bottles to give to people as Christmas presents, or you may decide to make a special homebrewed drink to celebrate a wedding, or just for a party, a BBQ, or to enjoy at home. Making fermented alcoholic drinks can be a good way to make the most of the fruits that you grow in your garden or pick from farmer's markets.

While brewing alcohol is technically fermenting, the process is obviously a bit different than fermenting vegetables, for example. You will also need some equipment specifically for brewing alcohol, all of which will be covered below.

Alcoholic Fermentation Basics

The alcohol in alcoholic drinks is a by-product of alcoholic fermentation, also known as ethyl alcohol fermentation. It's a biological process where yeast converts sugar into alcohol and carbon dioxide. Oxygen is not necessary for this, which means that alcoholic fermentation is an anaerobic process.

As yeast converts sugar into alcohol, it also creates carbon dioxide and heat, which raises the temperature of the fermenting produce. The yeast will keep eating the sugar until it's all gone or until the alcohol content in the mixture reaches around 16%. Above that level, the alcohol will kill the yeast and stop it from converting any more sugars.

Brewing alcohol at home is not difficult at all, and while you need some specialist equipment for that, it's nothing too crazy and won't cost you an arm and a leg. In fact, you can assemble a great setup for around $150, which will allow you to make your own wine, beer, mead, cider, and other alcoholic beverages.

Equipment Needed for Brewing Alcohol

- Fermentation vessel (fermenter)—there are many different types, but carboys are most commonly used for brewing alcohol at home. For smaller batches, a 1-gallon (3.8L) carboy is fine, but if you want to make bigger batches of beverages, you can consider getting a larger one.

- Airlock and bung—an airlock is inserted in the lid of a fermenter and allows carbon dioxide to escape without letting contaminants in. Depending on the fermenter, a bung is sometimes needed to secure the airlock. Without an airlock, the pressure in the fermenter could cause the lid or bung to pop off, or worse, the fermenter to explode, leaving you with a sad mess. Using an airlock is really easy—

you just need to fill your airlock up to the line with water and place it into the airtight gasket in the cap of your carboy.

- Auto siphon or racking cane and tubing—a siphon is a great way to streamline moving your brew or finished product around without the hassle and mess of lifting and pouring large quantities by hand. An auto siphon is essentially a more advanced version of a racking cane that also includes a pump and a filter, making it much easier to use, and I would personally recommend that you use that.

- Large pot—aluminum lobster pots work great for this. Again, the size will depend on how much alcohol you want to make at a time.

- Heat source—you need a heat source to heat the pot full of liquid. In most cases, the stove in your kitchen will be fine. You can consider getting a turkey fryer or another powerful heat source for larger batches.

- Hydrometer and hydrometer jar—a hydrometer is required for measuring the gravity of your beverages, which will allow you to figure out whether they are ready as well as their alcohol content. The jar is used for holding a sample of your beverage while taking gravity readings.

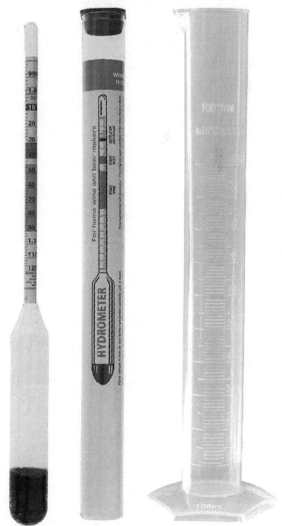

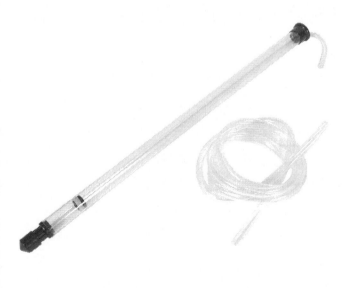

Flip top bottles—for bottling your beverages.

- Food grade sanitizer, either iodine based or acid based (I personally prefer Star San)—this is required for sanitizing all your equipment.

Determining the Alcohol Content Using a Hydrometer

A hydrometer measures the density of a liquid in relation to water. It's essentially a glass bulb that is weighted and floats in a testing jar. The hydrometer will tell you approximately how much alcohol was made in the fermentation process. In the case of brewing alcohol, we are measuring the amount of dissolved sugars in the brew to water. Pure water has a specific gravity of 1.000, and as sugars are dissolved into solution, it will cause the gravity to increase. Yeast will eat the sugar and convert it to alcohol, so a hydrometer can give you an estimated alcohol percentage that was produced in the fermentation process. You need to take the starting gravity reading right after preparing the recipe—you will need it later to calculate the alcohol content of your beverage.

How to Use a Hydrometer

1. Pour the sample liquid into the hydrometer jar.
2. Place the hydrometer in the jar, and give it a quick twirl to dislodge any air bubbles.
3. Once the hydrometer has settled, take the reading from the appropriate scale at the lowest level of the liquid's surface. Most liquids will cling slightly to the sides of the jar, giving their surfaces a slight downward curved called a meniscus.
4. Determine the temperature of your sample. If the temperature is different from the solution temperature of the hydrometer, use a temperature correction table from the instrument's manufacturer to adjust the readout. Many hydrometers are calibrated to a solution temperature of 60°F (15°C).

You can work out the alcohol content of your beverages with the following formula:

Alcohol % = (starting gravity − final gravity) x 131.25

Example: (1.050 − 1.000) x 131.25 = 6.5%

Stabilizing and Back Sweetening Homemade Wine

One of the most common issues you'll face when making homemade wine is that the wine you make is simply too dry. Most homemade fruit wines use sugar as the primary fermentable. Plain sugar is 100% fermentable, so when the yeast ferments the wine, all of the sugar gets converted to alcohol, leaving no residual sweetness. It's possible to back sweeten homemade wine, but you'll need to stabilize it first in order to ensure that the added sugar (or other sweeteners) doesn't start a second fermentation.

You can stabilize your wine once the fermentation has completely finished. You can check this using a hydrometer—in most cases, fruit wines are done fermenting when the gravity is below 0.998–1.000. To stabilize wine, you'll need potassium sorbate and Campden tablets (sodium metabisulphite). Potassium sorbate is an additive used extensively in the food industry as a preservative. It's used to prevent the growth of mold and yeast. It doesn't kill the yeast but stops it from reproducing. This means any live yeast will continue to ferment any sugars available but won't be able to reproduce new yeast cells. This is why we need to completely finish fermentation before stabilizing the wine. Campden tablets (sodium metabisulphite) are used as a disinfectant, preservative, and antioxidant in food. They inhibit the yeast and also prevent oxidization in the wine, which helps stabilize the flavor and color of the wine.

Once you've tried your wine and tested it with a hydrometer and you know it's ready to be stabilized, you can transfer it from its original fermenter into a new, clean vessel. Now you can add potassium sorbate and Campden tablets. You'll need ¾ teaspoon of potassium sorbate and 1 Campden tablet for each gallon (3.8L) of wine. Dissolve the additives in a small amount of boiled and cooled water until clear, then add the solution and mix gently. Leave the wine for at least 12 hours before doing anything else.

There are a few options available for back sweetening wine. The simplest is using sugar—simply dissolve it in water in 1:1 ratio, and pour the mixture into the wine. You can also use fruit juice. Grape juice is often used for this, and it adds a lovely flavor and sweetness to homemade wines. You can also use glycerin. It's a liquid that is colorless, flavorless, and odorless, and it tastes really sweet, plus it's unfermentable,

which is great. It's sold in home brew shops as wine sweetener.

There isn't "one size fits all" approach when back sweetening wine, so you'll have to try and test to see what works best for your wine and your taste. Simply take a small sample of wine (3.4 oz or 100 ml) and a small amount of the sweetener you're going to use. Then add a few drops of the sweetener, and taste test the wine. Keep adding the sweetener and sampling the wine to see when you reach the level of sweetness that works for you. Now you can extrapolate out the amount of sugar to the whole batch—one drop is 0.05 ml or 0.0017 oz. It's not an exact science, but this method will give you a rough amount to aim for. However, always be careful because you can't really dry out an oversweetened wine.

Alcoholic Beverages Recipes

1. Ginger Wine with Pea Flowers

This is a lovely ginger wine that is sparkling and has a fiery kick from the ginger. It's nice and warming, so it can make a nice drink to have on a cold winter evening. This recipe uses butterfly pea flowers, which make the wine have a vibrant purple color. The yeast used in the recipe is champagne yeast, which will create a drink that has approximately 16% alcohol.

Equipment

- Carboy with airlock (1 gallon or 3.8L)
- Large glass fermentation jar
- Large saucepan or stockpot
- Fine filter bag
- Funnel
- Auto siphon or racking cane and tubing
- Pressure-resistant glass bottles

- 2 tablespoon Star San sanitizer

Ingredients

- 14 cups (3.36L) filtered water
- 4½ cups (900 g) sugar
- 1 cup (50 g) butterfly pea flowers
- 1 sachet champagne yeast
- ½ cup (50 g) fresh ginger

Instructions

1. Clean the kitchen sink, and secure the plug. Fill the sink ¾ full with cold water. Pour in 2 tablespoons of Star San sanitizer.

2. Immerse the jar, carboy, and funnel. Let it stand for 2 minutes, then drain. No rinsing required.

3. Dissolve the contents of the yeast sachet in a glass of lukewarm water, and place it to one side.

4. Chop the ginger very finely (or use a food processor).

5. Add the ginger, sugar, and 2 cups (480 ml) of water to a large saucepan.

6. Heat the pan on high, stirring constantly until the sugar dissolves. Once it reaches boiling, then reduce the heat and simmer for 10 minutes.

7. Take the pan off the heat, add in the pea flowers, and let them infuse for 5 minutes.

8. Filter the liquid through a fine mesh sieve.

9. Add 12 cups (2.88L) of cold, filtered water to dilute the sugar and ginger mixture.

10. Add the reactivated yeast to the jar.

11. Pour the contents of the jar into the carboy using the funnel.

12. Fill the airlock with water up to the line, then fit the stopper and airlock onto the carboy.

13. Ferment at room temperature until there is less than 1 airlock bubble per minute (for 1 to 1.5 months).

14. Next, place the carboy in the fridge for 24 hours—this will clarify the liquid (it's known as cold crash concept).

15. Then transfer the ginger wine to the bottles with the auto siphon, ensuring that you don't put any of the deposits at the bottom.

16. Let these bottles ferment for 2 weeks at room temperature.

17. The wine at this point is fine to be drunk immediately, but if you were to age it a few months at room temperature, it would taste even better.

18. Enjoy chilled over ice, or add it to cocktails.

2. Rhubarb Wine

If you grow your own rhubarb in your garden or backyard, there's only so many rhubarb crumbles you can eat! But rhubarb makes for a delicious, tangy, sharp, and beautiful drink, and it's especially nice as wine. This will create a dry, slightly sparkling wine, and the alcohol content will be approximately 10%. You can use frozen rhubarb for this recipe too. So, if you have a big harvest of rhubarb and wish to freeze some, you can make this wine at any time of the year from it.

Equipment

- Wide mouth glass jar with lid
- Large saucepan
- Carboy with pierced lid and airlock (1 gallon or 3.8L)
- Auto siphon
- Funnel
- Nylon filter
- Hydrometer (optional)
- Flip top glass bottles
- 1 teaspoon Star San sanitizer

Ingredients

- 1 gallon (3.8L) filtered water
- 3.3 lb (1.5 kg) rhubarb
- 2.2 lb (1 kg) sugar
- 2 bags plain black tea
- 1 sachet K1 yeast
- ¼ teaspoon Fermaid yeast nutrient

Instructions

1. Rinse the rhubarb, and remove any damaged parts. Chop the rhubarb into 1-inch (2.5 cm) pieces. Place the rhubarb in the jar.
2. Add the sugar, and put the lid on the jar.
3. Let the syrup macerate. Stir it once a day to help the sugar dissolve.
4. After 7 days, use a fine mesh to sieve out the rhubarb, and pour the remaining syrup into a saucepan.
5. Put the rhubarb pieces back in the jar, cover with ½ gallon (1.9L) of water, and stir to get as much syrup out as possible. Strain again and pour into the saucepan.
6. Heat the saucepan, and remove it from the heat as soon as it starts to boil.
7. Add in the black tea to the syrup, and let it infuse for 10 minutes, then remove the tea bags.
8. You can use the rhubarb pieces to make jam, pie, or muffins so that there is no waste.
9. Add the sanitizer to the carboy. Fill the carboy up to the brim with cold water and leave for 2 minutes.
10. Clean your sink. Put the contents of the carboy into the sink.
11. Soak any equipment you will use, such as a funnel, pierced lid, airlock, auto siphon, hydrometer, etc. Allow the sanitizer product to work for 2 minutes, and don't rinse, just drain.

12. In a small bowl, dissolve the yeast in ¼ cup (60 ml) of warm water.

13. Once the rhubarb syrup has cooled to below 104°F (40°C), then you can add in the yeast and yeast nutrient mix and stir with a spoon.

14. Pour the liquid into the carboy using the funnel.

15. Top up with water, leaving 2 inches (5 cm) of space from the rim.

16. Dip the hydrometer into the carboy. It should read around 1.075.

17. Put the pierced lid on the carboy. Push the auto siphon tube into the hole. Put the other end of the tube in a glass filled with water.

18. Ferment for 5 days at room temperature out of direct sunlight. The fermentation will be very active.

19. Replace the auto siphon tube with the airlock. Fill the airlock with water up to the line.

20. Ferment for 3 more weeks or until no more bubbles appear in the airlock.

21. You can age the rhubarb wine for a few more months in the carboy.

22. Sanitize the bottles, auto siphon, and hydrometer. The hydrometer reading should ideally be 0.998. If the gravity is higher than 1.005, let it ferment for a few more weeks.

23. Fill up the bottles, leaving 1 inch (2.5 cm) of space from the top. Ensure you don't put any of the bottom deposits from the carboy into the bottles. You can add 1 teaspoon of white sugar for every 25 oz (750 ml) of wine to make sparkling wine.

24. Close the bottles, and leave them for 2 weeks somewhere dark.

25. You can drink the rhubarb wine immediately, but it tastes even better if you let it age for 6 months.

3. Zesty Orange Wine

Orange wine is not as popular as some of the other fruit wines, but it can make a great early evening sipper. You can make this recipe with oranges, tangerines, mandarins, or blood oranges.

Equipment

- Large stockpot
- Small fermenting bucket
- Carboy
- Airlock and bung
- Auto siphon
- Fine straining bag
- Potato masher
- Sanitizer

Ingredients

- 3.3 lb (1.5 kg) oranges
- 2.2 lb (1 kg) orange blossom honey
- 1 gallon (3.8Ł) water
- 1 sachet yeast
- 1 teaspoon yeast nutrient
- ¼ teaspoon wine tannin
- ½ teaspoon pectic enzyme
- 1 Campden tablet (sodium metabisulfite)

Instructions

1. Peel the zest off half of your oranges with a potato peeler to get large pieces of zest, avoiding the white pith.

2. Peel and segment the oranges.

3. Sanitize the equipment you will be using.

4. Place the zest and orange segments into a straining bag.

5. Put the straining bag into the sanitized fermenter.

6. Heat half the water in a large pan. Bring it to a boil, then remove from heat.

7. Add honey to the hot water, stir, then pour over the fruit in the fermenting vessel. Stir and add remaining half of cold water.

8. Add the crushed Campden tablet and leave covered for 12 hours.

9. Next, add the yeast nutrient, wine tannin, and pectic enzyme and stir. Leave this for 24 hours.

10. Add the yeast by sprinkling it on the surface (you can rehydrate the yeast by following the packet instructions).

11. Cover the liquid, fit an airlock, and allow to ferment. Stir every day to circulate the fruit.

12. After 7 days, lift the straining bag out, and allow it drain to thoroughly, but don't squeeze out any liquid.

13. Cover the fermenting vessel, and allow it to settle for 24 hours.

14. Pour the wine into the carboy. You can use a hydrometer to measure the starting gravity so that you can determine the alcohol content of your wine later. Fit a bung and airlock, and allow the fermentation to complete.

15. Over months, the wine will clear. You will see sediment has built up at the bottom of the carboy after about a month. This means it's time to siphon your wine into a new, clean vessel. Repeat this whenever you have a lot of sediment.

16. After approximately 4 months, the wine will have cleared, and you can bottle it. You can measure the gravity with the hydrometer now to figure out the alcohol content. Sample the wine, and if you want to sweeten it, you can do so.

4. Berry Mead

This is a delicious dry and fizzy berry mead. It has an alcohol content of about 10% and a fruity taste that is light and sparkling. Mead is also sometimes called honey wine. There are different types of mead, and this one is a melomel (the name for mead that contains fruit). This berry mead contains blueberries, blackberries, and raspberries.

Equipment

- Carboy with airlock (1 gallon or 3.8L)
- Large glass fermentation jar
- Funnel
- Auto siphon
- Kitchen whisk

- Hydrometer
- Pressure resistant glass bottles
- 2 tablespoons Star San sanitizer

Ingredients

- 14 cups (3.36L) filtered water
- ⅔ cup (100 g) frozen blueberries
- ⅔ cup (100 g) frozen raspberries
- ⅔ cup (100 g) frozen blackberries
- 2.2 lb (1 kg) clover honey
- 1 sachet champagne yeast
- Yeast food (optional)

Instructions

1. Clean the kitchen sink, and secure the plug. Fill the sink ¾ full. Put in 2 tablespoons of Star San sanitizer.

2. Immerse the jar, carboy, funnel, and whisk. Leave them in contact with the sanitizer for 2 minutes—you don't need to rinse this off.

3. Put the contents of the yeast sachet in a glass of lukewarm water, then place this to one side.

4. Pour the water and honey into the large fermentation jar.

5. Use the whisk to ensure the honey has thoroughly dissolved.

6. Place the yeast in the jar, and give it a good mix.

7. Pour the contents of the jar into the carboy using the funnel.

8. Fit the lid and airlock, and fill the airlock with water to the line.

9. Let this ferment at room temperature until there is less than 1 airlock bubble per minute (it usually takes about 1–2 months).

10. Crush the berries with a blender.

11. Pour the fruit puree into the fermentation jar.

12. Get the mead from the carboy to the fermentation jar, leaving as much sediment as possible at the bottom of the carboy.

13. Put the lid on the jar and place in the fridge for 2 weeks.

14. Pour the mead from the jar to the bottles, ensuring you don't transfer any fruit residue.

15. Let the bottles stand for a month at room temperature to allow natural carbonation to take place.

16. After this time, the mead is ready to drink. But if you let it age for a year or two at room temperature away from light, the flavor will improve further.

5. Maple Mead

This recipe is made with honey, maple syrup, and spices, and it's warming and delightful. There are many types of mead, and this one is called acerglyn because it's made with maple syrup. This mead has a warming feel, which is perfect for the colder months. After 1 month of fermentation, it should have approximately 5% alcohol content.

Equipment

- Large pot
- Long-handled spoon
- Large funnel
- 1-gallon (3.8L) carboy with pierced lid and airlock
- Auto siphon with tubing
- Bottling wand
- Thermometer
- Flip top bottles
- Sanitizer

Ingredients

- 12 cups (2.88L) filtered water
- 3 cups (1,020 g) maple syrup
- 1 cup (340 g) honey
- 1 orange, washed and cut into thin slices
- ¼ cup (38 g) raisins
- 1 cinnamon stick
- 4 cloves
- ¼ packet champagne yeast

Instructions

1. Clean and sanitize the equipment and work surfaces.
2. Put the maple syrup, honey, cinnamon, cloves, and raisins in a saucepan. Heat them very gently, just allowing them to have a gentle simmer for 15 minutes.
3. Take the saucepan off the heat, add 4 cups (960 ml) of water, and stir well.
4. Use a funnel to pour the saucepan's contents into the carboy, and add in the orange slices.
5. Cover with the remaining cold water, leaving 2 inches (5 cm) of space at the top.
6. In a small bowl, rehydrate the champagne yeast in ¼ cup (60 ml) of warm water, and add this yeast to the carboy.
7. Close it with the pierced lid and airlock. Ensure you fill the airlock with water to the line.
8. Let this ferment for 4 weeks at room temperature until the airlock no longer has any bubbles.
9. Bottle the mead in pressure-resistant bottles.
10. While you can drink the mead immediately, if you let it age for 6 months, it will have a much better taste.

6. Hard Apple Cider

Making hard apple cider is probably one of the best ways to preserve apples. This recipe will give you an apple cider that has approximately 5% alcohol.

Equipment

- Large pot
- Funnel
- 1-gallon (3.8L) carboy with cap and airlock
- Auto siphon
- Thermometer
- Bottling wand
- Flip top bottles
- Sanitizer

Ingredients

- 1 gallon (3.8L) fresh, unfiltered apple juice without preservatives
- 1 lb (450 g) brown sugar

- ½ packet champagne yeast
- 1 cinnamon stick
- 3 cloves
- 10 raisins

Instructions

1. Clean and sanitize all the equipment you will need.

2. Heat ½ gallon (1.9L) of apple juice in a pot on medium heat, but don't boil.

3. Add the brown sugar and stir until it has dissolved, then remove the pot from the heat.

4. Put the cinnamon stick, cloves, and raisins into the carboy.

5. Use the funnel to transfer the warm cider from the pot into the carboy. Allow the warm cider to steep with the spices for about 20 minutes.

6. Top off the carboy with the remaining ½ gallon (1.9L) of apple juice, leaving 2 inches (5 cm) of space at the top. You will have a bit leftover apple juice.

7. Put the cap on the carboy, and shake it to combine everything.

8. Use a thermometer to check the temperature of the juice in the carboy. When it has cooled to 90°F (32°C) or less, you can add ½ packet of yeast (doesn't have to be exact). You can store the opened package with the remaining yeast in the fridge for later use.

9. Cap the carboy again and shake vigorously for about a minute or two to aerate the yeast.

10. Attach the airlock to the rubber stopper, fill it with water to the line, then place it firmly on the top of the carboy.

11. Put the jug in a cool (but not cold) place out of direct sunlight to ferment. After a few hours, you will start to see bubbles forming in the carboy and airlock.

12. Allow the cider to ferment for 3–4 weeks until the bubbling has stopped.

13. You can bottle the cider now. Enjoy!

7. Apple Cyser Mead

A cyser is a blend between an apple cider and a mead. Fermenting the fruit and honey combination is also referred to as melomel, but the apple and honey base has earned its own name. Cider is traditionally made from apple juice, and mead is just honey and water, also known as hydromel. This magnificent blend of these two delicious recipes makes a fine drink that is sure to disappear quickly if you are patient enough to handle the long aging process. Apple cyser can be a great drink if you are looking for a higher alcohol content than traditional cider along with complimentary honey and floral flavors. You will need some apple cider from the previous recipe for this one. Because of the higher alcohol content, this cyser recipe will require a few months of aging to mellow the alcohol and bring out the flavor.

Equipment

- Cleanser and sanitizer
- Carboy
- Airlock
- Auto siphon
- Hydrometer
- Bottling bucket
- Flip top bottles

Ingredients

- 1 gallon apple cider (please see the previous recipe)
- 2 lb (900 g) honey
- 1 teaspoon yeast nutrient
- ½ teaspoon yeast energizer
- ¼ pack Lalvin 71b yeast

Instructions

1. Clean and sanitize all the equipment before starting.
2. Place the honey container in warm water to make it flow easier.
3. Pour the apple juice and honey into the carboy and mix.
4. Measure the gravity with the hydrometer, and make a record.
5. Add half of the yeast nutrient and energizer.
6. Pour the yeast into the carboy.
7. Close the carboy, and install the airlock filled with sanitizer.
8. After 1 day, add the second half of yeast nutrient and energizer.
9. Allow the cyser to ferment in a cool and dark place for about 6–8 weeks.
10. Refrigerate for 24 hours (cold crash), rack, and bottle.

8. Simple Homemade Beer

Making your own beer is not difficult at all, and it's not expensive either. This simple method uses just one fermenting process, so you will need only one brewing container. This recipe will give you about 6 gallons (23L) of lovely homemade beer.

Equipment

- Sanitizer (such as Star San)
- 10-gallon (38L) food grade plastic carboy with lid
- Siphon hose
- Hose clamp for siphon
- Twelve 2-liter plastic pop bottles with lids
- Hydrometer
- Thermometer

Ingredients

- 40 oz (1.2L) can malt extract, any flavor you like (light, dark, stout) (Or a 1.5 kg tall can of the same—it contains more malt extract, so you can make a larger batch or use the same method here to make a richer beer. You can also buy "pre-hopped" extract, which will impart more of a hop flavor to your beer.)
- 1 teaspoon brewers' yeast (some malt extracts come with little packets of yeast included)
- 8–9 cups (1.6–1.8 kg) corn sugar (preferred), or you can use 6–7 cups (1.2–1.4 kg) of regular white sugar
- Filtered water
- For even better results, consider using 2 cans of malt extract and not using any sugar. This will be more expensive but will enrich the taste of the beer.

Instructions

1. Sanitize all the equipment. First, clean everything with warm, lightly soapy water. Rinse well to remove soap residue. Then sanitize with a bleach solution (1 tablespoon per gallon (3.8L) of water). You can also use a no-rinse acid sanitizer, such as Star San, which is effective and leaves no aftertaste.

2. After you've cleaned and sanitized all your equipment, it's time to start brewing your beer! Pour 10.5 quarts (10L) of fresh, cold water into the carboy. If the carboy is new, wash it out first with a mixture of water and baking soda to remove the plastic smell.

3. In your largest pot, bring 7.3 quarts (7L) of water to a boil.

4. Add 1 can of malt extract. Stir and cook uncovered for 20 minutes.

5. Add the sugar and stir until it has dissolved.

6. As soon as the sugar has dissolved, pour the contents into the carboy. Pour the contents quickly because this will add air to the mixture. And the more air the yeast gets initially, the better. It allows the yeast to grow rapidly and get things going.

7. Top up with bottled drinking water until the temperature is neutral (you can use tap water, but it needs to be boiled for 15 minutes and left to stand for 24 hours in an open container first). Test using a clean, sanitized thermometer. The carboy will now be a little more than half full.

8. Sprinkle in the yeast and stir well. Cover with the lid. Set the lid on loosely because if the carboy is capped too tightly, it can explode from the carbon dioxide build up.

9. Keep the carboy covered, and avoid unnecessary opening. The beer will be ready to bottle in 6–10 days, depending on the temperature of the room and the amount of sugar used in the brewing. The temperature should be 68–75°F (20–24°C) at the highest; 61–68° (16–20°C) is better, but it will take the beer a day or two longer to ferment.

10. Test your beer readiness with a hydrometer. Set hydrometer into the beer, and spin it once to release bubbles (which can cling to it and give a false reading). Your beer is ready to bottle when the reading is 1.008 for dark beers and 1.010–1.015 for light beers. If you don't have a hydrometer, you can judge readiness by tasting a sample—it should not be sweet. There should be little or no bubbling in the beer.

11. When your beer is ready to bottle, set the carboy on a sturdy table and the twelve 2-liter bottles on the floor, with newspaper underneath to catch drips or overflows. Using a funnel, put 2 level teaspoons of sugar in each bottle.

12. Siphon the beer into the bottles, trying not to disturb the sediment on the bottom of the carboy. You can tape a plastic straw alongside the bottom end of the siphon hose, with 1 inch (2.5 cm) projecting beyond the end. The tip of the straw can touch the bottom of the carboy without the siphon drawing up sediment. Tip the carboy as you near the bottom.

13. It's important to not splash or agitate the beer too much when bottling, as any oxygen introduced can lead to oxidation and a "cardboard" taste.

14. As you fill the bottles, keep the end of the siphon tube near the bottom of the bottle to avoid frothing. It is essential that the bottles are not completely filled—leave an inch or two (2.5–5 cm) of headspace. Screw the caps on tightly. Invert each bottle and shake to dissolve the sugar at the bottom. Set bottles in a warm area for the first few days, then store in a cool, dark place. You can

drink the beer within a few days of bottling, but it will improve with age.

9. Alcoholic Ginger Beer

This alcoholic ginger beer is made with a ginger bug. It's a delicious drink with a fiery kick of heat from ginger. It will have an alcohol content similar to beer, typically between 3 and 5%.

Equipment

- Jar with wide opening or carboy (1 gallon or 3.8L)
- Airlock
- Blender, food processor, or a good knife and some patience
- Zester/fine grater
- Sieve
- Pressure-resistant bottles
- Sanitizer

Ingredients

- ½ cup (120 ml) ginger bug (please see the home-made root beer recipe (number 8) from the previous chapter for instructions on how to make it)
- 12½ cups (3L) water
- 2 cups (400 g) sugar
- 2 lemons
- 1½ cups (150 g) ginger
- ½ cup (75 g) raisins
- Mint (optional)

Instructions

1. Sanitize all the equipment you will need.
2. Zest and juice the lemons. You can compost the peel.
3. Put all the ingredients into a blender with 2 cups (480 ml) of water and blend.
4. Filter the blended liquid with a fine sieve.
5. Pour the liquid into a clean jar, and top with water, leaving 1 inch (2.5 cm) of space at the top.
6. Put a lid on the jar that has an airlock.
7. Fill the airlock to the line with water or alcohol.
8. Allow this to ferment at room temperature until no more bubbles appear. Usually, this takes 1–3 months.
9. Transfer the ginger beer into pressure-resistant bottles, ensuring you leave the sediment at the bottom of the jar.
10. Keep these bottles in the dark for 1 month—this will help them to sparkle and for the flavors to become more intense.
11. While this is ready to drink immediately, if you can leave it for several months, the taste will be even better.

10. Mexican Pulque

This is a traditional Mexican fermented alcoholic drink from central Mexico. It's similar to beer. It's made from fermented sap from agave. It's thick, gooey, with a milky sweet yeasty flavor. It has a short shelf life, and if any is left over, it's discarded at the end of the day. It's a mixture between beer, yogurt, and juice.

Equipment

- Sanitizer
- Carboy
- Airlock
- Auto siphon
- Flip top bottles

Ingredients

- 4 gallons (15.2L) filtered water

- 8½ lb (3.85 kg) dark agave nectar

- 1 packet champagne yeast

- ½ oz (15 g) dried coriander seeds, crushed

Instructions

1. Sanitize all the equipment you will need.

2. Prime your champagne yeast 2 days beforehand.

3. Boil the water.

4. Once it reaches the boiling point, remove from heat, and add in the agave nectar. Add the crushed coriander seeds for some floral aroma. Boil for 20 more minutes. Then take off the heat and let it cool.

5. Once the liquid has cooled, pour it into the carboy. Cover it with the lid, and install the airlock—remember to fill it with water to the line.

6. Ferment it for 3 weeks, and then allow a further week for the sweetness to develop (this is personal taste).

7. When pulque is fresh, it will have an alcohol content of 2–4%. If it's a little older, it will taste sourer and have a 5–7% alcohol content.

We have a lot of apple trees on our homestead, so every fall we make hard cider to help preserve the massive harvest of apples we get every year. It's easy to make, and it's delicious on a cold winter evening. We also make some cyser using the cider later in the winter.

Key takeaways from this chapter:

1. You will need some equipment to make alcohol: sanitizer, a carboy, a funnel, an airlock, flip top pressure-resistant bottles, yeast, yeast nutrient, and a hydrometer.

2. Adding butterfly pea flowers to your wine will give it a nice purple hue.

3. Champagne yeast is good to use for wine and mead.

4. Most alcohol tastes better if you age it for a few months in a dark place.

5. There are different types of mead—melomel (fruit) and acerglyn (maple syrup).

6. When transferring alcohol from a carboy into bottles, be careful not to pour any of the deposit from the bottom of the container.

Conclusion

This concludes the book on pickling and fermenting for beginners. The book started out with an introduction to pickling and how it works. It discussed the key differences between pickling and fermenting (pickling is done using an acidic brine, like vinegar, whereas fermentation happens due to a chemical reaction between sugars in the food and naturally present bacteria that turn the sugars to acetic acid, which in turn helps preserve the produce). It mentioned the type of tools and equipment that may come in useful. It also discussed in detail the three different types of fermentation. After that, the book moves on to lots of different pickling and fermenting recipes.

There's a chapter on quick pickles, with a wide variety of recipes for quick pickling different vegetables and fruits. Then there's a chapter on fermented pickles with recipes like fermented garlic, fermented red onions, and fermented sugar snap peas, among many others. Next is a chapter specifically on fruit and sweet pickles with some amazingly delicious recipes. Chapter 6 focuses on sauerkraut, kimchi, and other cabbage recipes. Chapter 7 covers a wide array of salsas, hot sauces, chutneys, relishes, and other condiments. Chapter 8 is a little unusual and includes recipes for pickled and fermented meats, fish, and eggs. This interesting chapter contains recipes for corned beef, Cape Malay pickled fish, and beautiful beet pickled eggs with cardamom and anise (which are bright pink and look stunning), among many others.

The final two chapters of the book are really interesting and cover fermented beverages, both non-alcoholic, so drinks like blackberry switchel, kombucha, kvass, tepache, kefir, and soda, and alcoholic drinks, such as wine, mead, cider, beer, and pulque.

I hope that this book has shown you that pickling and fermentation is really diverse and there is something for everyone, whether you want to pickle or ferment vegetables, fruits, meat, fish, or eggs, or make drinks, sauces, sauerkraut, or relishes. Wherever your interest lies with pickling or fermentation, there will surely be a recipe that takes your interest and inspires you to give this a try. Pickling and fermenting are a wonderful way to preserve food and make outstanding use of your garden, homestead, or backyard harvests. When you pickle and ferment, you can preserve food to eat later throughout the year. It also makes for some wonderful, unique, and thoughtful gifts that you can give to friends and family.

Now that you've finished reading the book, my advice would be to gather the equipment you need to pickle and ferment. Ensure you have sterilized everything properly, gather your ingredients, and start pickling and fermenting and enjoying what you create!

Altitude Adjustments

It's important to take your home's altitude into consideration when you are canning foods to preserve them. You may need to make some adjustments. At higher altitudes, water boils at a lower temperature because the air is thinner.

You need to know the elevation of where you live. It may possibly be higher than you presume. You can check your altitude online or with your county extension office. Then you can adjust your processing times if you are canning your produce.

Home Canning Altitude Adjustments for Water Bath Canning

When you're using a boiling water canner, you can use the following adjustments as a guideline:

- At 1,001–3,000 feet (305–915 m) above sea level, increase processing time by 5 minutes.

- At 3,001–6,000 (915–1,830 m) feet above sea level, increase processing time by 10 minutes.

- At 6,001–8,000 (1,830–2.440 m) feet above sea level, increase processing time by 15 minutes.

- At 8,001–10,000 (2,440–3,050 m) feet above sea level, increase processing time by 20 minutes.

Blanching Food or Sterilizing Jars

For blanching, add 1 minute if you live 5,000 feet (1,525 m) or more above sea level. For sterilizing jars, boil them an additional minute for each 1,000 feet (305 m) above sea level.

Resources

Pickling

Bonem, Max. 2017. The Science of Vinegar Pickling, Explained. *Food & Wine*. Online.

https://www.foodandwine.com/vegetables/pickled-vegetables/science-vinegar-pickles-explained

Dunston, Lara. N.d. Beginners Guide to Pickling – How to Pickle Almost Anything. *Grantourismo*. Online. https://grantourismotravels.com/beginners-guide-to-pickling/

Ferroli, Christina. 2022. How to Make Pickles: Step-by-Step Pickling Guide. *Almanac*. 13th June 2022. Online. https://www.almanac.com/how-to-pickle

Home & Garden Information Center. 2012. Pickle Basics. *Home & Garden Information Center*. Online. 20th March 2012. https://hgic.clemson.edu/factsheet/pickle-basics/

Houston, Gillie. 2018. The Beginner's Guide to Pickling. *My Recipes*. Online. 31st January 2018. https://www.myrecipes.com/how-to/beginners-guide-to-pickling

Mountain Feed. N.d. Home Pickling Basics – What You Need to Know to Get Started. *MountainFeed*. Online. https://www.mountainfeed.com/blogs/learn/15816841-home-pickling-basics-what-you-need-to-know-to-get-started

Mrs Wheelbarrow. 2014. Mrs. Wheelbarrow's 9 Essential Tools for Pickling and Preserving. *Food52*. Online. 2nd July 2014. https://food52.com/blog/10727-mrs-wheelbarrow-s-9-essential-tools-for-pickling-and-preserving

University of Minnesota Extension. 2021. Pickling Basics. Online. https://extension.umn.edu/preserving-and-preparing/pickling-basics

Fermenting

Alfaro, Danilo. 2022. What is Fermentation? The 3 Types Used for Food and Beverage. *The Spruce Eats*. Online. 13th May 2022.

https://www.thespruceeats.com/what-is-fermentation-5220493

Coyle, Daisy. 2020. What is Fermentation? The Lowdown on Fermented Foods. *Healthline*. 20th August 2020. Online.

https://www.healthline.com/nutrition/fermentation

Driessen, Suzanne. 2022. How to Make Fermented Pickles. *University of Minnesota Extension*. Online. https://extension.umn.edu/preserving-and-preparing/how-make-fermented-pickles

Eat Cultured. 2018. Fermentation: The Basics. *Eat Cultured*. Online. 22nd February 2018.

https://eatcultured.com/blogs/our-awesome-blog/fermentation-the-basics

Northern Homestead. 2022. Fermenting is Simple – Learn the Basics. *Northern Homestead*. Online. https://northernhomestead.com/fermenting-simple/

Plantables. 2019. Fermenting 101: Everything You Need to Know About Pickling, Fermenting and Brewing Your Own Food, *Plantables*. Online. 15th March 2019. https://plantables.ca/fermenting-101-everything-you-need-to-know-about-pickling-fermenting-and-brewing-your-own-food/

Reddin, Dorothy. 2021. Kate Middleton gifted Queen her 'granny's recipe of chutney' – 'shows her thoughtfulness' *Daily Express*. 23rd October 2021. Online. https://www.express.co.uk/life-style/food/1509778/kate-middleton-chutney-recipe-christmas-gift-queen

Sensorex. 2021. The Fermentation Process Explained. *Sensorex*. Online.

https://sensorex.com/2021/11/16/the-fermentation-process-explained/

Alcoholic Fermentation

Maria C. Hunt. 2023. Alcoholic Fermentation: What Is It, and Why Is It Important? *Wine Enthusiast.* Online. May 9th 2023.

https://www.wineenthusiast.com/basics/how-its-made/alcoholic-fermentation/

University of Georgia Extension. 2013. Winemaking at Home. Online. January 18th 2013.

https://extension.uga.edu/publications/detail.html?number=C717&title=winemaking-at-home

Eartheasy. N.d. Simplest Homemade Beer. Online. https://learn.eartheasy.com/guides/simplest-homemade-beer/

Canning

Moranville, Winni. 2022. Necessary Canning Adjustments for High Altitudes. Online. https://www.bhg.com/recipes/how-to/preserving-canning/altitude-adjustments/

USDA. N.d. Complete Guide to Home Canning. Guide 6. Preparing and Canning Fermented Foods and Pickled Vegetables. *USDA.* Online.

https://nchfp.uga.edu/publications/usda/GUIDE06_HomeCan_rev0715.pdf

Recipes

Mitts, Gigi. 2019. 30 Fermented Drinks You Can Make at Home. *My Fermented Foods.* Online. 15th June 2019. https://myfermentedfoods.com/fermented-drinks/

Modern Day Self Reliance. 2021. 28 Easy Fermentation Recipes. *Modern Day Self Reliance.* 14th June 2021. Online.

https://moderndayselfreliance.com/28-easy-fermentation-recipes/

Ngo, Irene. 2022. 21 Easy Quick Pickle Recipes to Make the Most of All That Produce. *Chatelaine.* Online. 14th September 2022.

https://www.chatelaine.com/recipes/recipe-collections/quick-pickles-recipes/

Revolution Fermentation. N.d. Fermented Beverages Recipes. Online.

https://revolutionfermentation.com/en/blogs/category/fermented-beverages/beverages-recipes/

Robicelli, Allison. 2022. 32 Must-Try Pickling Recipes. *Taste of Home.* Online. 18th July 2022. https://www.tasteofhome.com/collection/pickled-recipes/

Index

Recipes page numbers are marked in **bold**

Made in United States
Troutdale, OR
11/19/2024

25080854R00075